Is it Easier to Kill or Write a Poem?

Is it Easier to Kill or Write a Poem?

WRITTEN BY A GREEN BERET

Barry Lloyd Grissom

ISBN: 0692684018
ISBN 13: 9780692684016
Library of Congress Control Number: 2016906025
Maritta's Book Sales, Fayetteville NC

Dedicated to my soul mate, Maritta, my son and daughter, David and Elizabeth, and my mother and father, all of whom are my unit, now and forever.

Introduction

My name is Sergeant Major (Retired) Barry L. Grissom. I was in the army for twenty-eight years and in the US Army Special Forces for twenty-three of that. Before I begin telling my story, I would like to put forth the following disclaimer to put my community's mind at ease. I am not writing this book to tell wild stories about my adventures in Central or South America—or anywhere else I have been in the world—while serving my country. I am writing primarily for myself, for writing therapy; and if, in the process, I am able to help another unfortunate soul, then it was meant to be. I am well on the path to a happy and healthy life, and if I can help guide one person toward the same then I will have accomplished my task. I will not discuss politics, mention names, nor discriminate against others or myself. For those who have been involved in some way with me during my life, they will know when they are mentioned; the average reader will not.

I am an alcoholic, and I have been for a very long time. I can never remember being a social drinker. I always drank to forget, even when I didn't know what I was forgetting. I would need to drink to drown my constant headaches or, sometimes, just because everybody else was doing it.! I never needed an excuse to drink. I would just drink anyway. While this is not going to be one of those Alcohol Anonymous stories, it is the story of my life, and unfortunately alcohol was a major part of it. I have never told my entire story to anyone, not even to my beautiful wife, and I am not going to disclose every last detail in this book. While I have talked to myriad people over the last few years, they have each only seen bits and glimpses of me. This is just another part of my story.

CHAPTER 1

Beginnings

had some significant childhood trauma. There was stress and violence. More than the average person in some cases, less in others. I have always known something wasn't quite right but have always done an excellent job burying memories deep and out of reach. Unfortunately, like from *The Wall*, the album by Pink Floyd, memories do tend to reemerge, consciously or subconsciously, sometimes as passing remembrances, sometimes in dreams, sometimes all of it flooding in like from a broken dam after you have hit rock bottom. I was a jumbled mess after I got the alcohol out of my system, sobered up, and decided to stay that way. My dreams were vivid, confusing, and horrifying. But as one of my friends once said, "Better living through chemistry!"

My alcohol intake is now replaced with a drug that helps me forget those dreams, but at the time, I couldn't differentiate memories. My dreams and thoughts were a horrid mixture from my childhood, the many deaths I dealt with—family or fallen comrades—mixed with a Dean Koontz–like story line that always involved rape and violence. The images were all so vivid that I thought I was there. I wasn't making much headway with the therapy sessions the army put me in until my therapist suggested I talk to my mother about what happened to me when I was a child. She convinced me that I had to get the story from her. After all, that is where it all began. I definitely had mixed feelings about this. We had never had such a discussion before.

My mother is a nurse practitioner with an alphabet of qualifications following her name. I never really knew what she did for a living until I got my own personal "pill doc," or at least that was what I liked to call them. There is an interesting relationship between the therapist and the "pill doc"; one cannot exist without the other. I called her one night and found out quite a bit from our conversation. I had made a breakthrough. I was able to begin separating memories and dreams and place them in a sequence that began to make sense.

My biological father was unstable. I guess this is an understatement. I thank God today that I didn't get any of that tablespoon of crazy. I don't personally remember much about him, just bits and pieces of experiences, and I have never met him as an adult, nor will I ever. He became my mother's stalker when she decided he had to go. I was around seven years old. My mom helped me to remember two concrete experiences. The first was at my grandparents' home in Tallmadge, Ohio. He had followed my mother and blocked her in my grandparents' long, gravel driveway when she returned one day. He then approached the house to take her and my sister and me. My grandmother, bless her heart, unloaded two shotgun barrels of salt rock into him. I remember the flash and noise, the ringing in the ears.

The next one was six months later; I vaguely remember standing in a doorway with my biological father, pistol in his hand, holding my sister staring out at the flashing red-and-blue lights and bright headlights. They came to arrest him for kidnapping us. That episode had begun with us returning home one day. I somewhat remember my mother panicking because all the doorknobs were removed from the doors on the inside of the house. He came and got us, and the adventure began, driving us from state to state, motel to motel, until the drugs couldn't keep him awake anymore. My mother escaped out of the bathroom window and sent the police to get him and rescue us.

My mother was only with her second husband for less than a year. He was a mean drunk. I remember the nights in the bars, particularly the one that had a bowling game. The pins were on wires, and you rolled a puck down the board. He drank all the time and beat my sister and me with a hairbrush. He didn't care about leaving marks. I guess it didn't matter much back then. Not good times for any of us.

However, God works in mysterious ways and eventually brought my mom together with her current husband. He was and still is a recovering alcoholic. He is a good man, and hasn't drank in over forty years. He even sent me his leather Alcohol Anonymous binder while I was in rehab, which I still have today. He is the only one that I consider my father, and they are still married today.

I would have another life change soon after they got married in Ohio. My first drink was a can of Budweiser. I must have been ten or eleven years old. I played baseball in Ohio, and I remember my coach bringing a cooler full of beer. We all drank one. I will never forget how good it tasted. Jane Fonda wasn't married to Ted Turner at the time, so I hadn't started boycotting Budweiser yet. Unfortunately, it gave me a bad trip because I was on Ritalin and Dexedrine for ADHD at the time. I was a bit out of control as a kid—imagine that. My family didn't have a lot of money, but we lived comfortably. I was going to find out soon, though, that I had lived a sheltered life. Except, of course, for all the crazy stuff I've already mentioned.

We moved to Phoenix, Arizona, when I was in middle school and moved into a large apartment complex. Day-to-day life was normal, but outside the complex it was a jungle of gangs and violence. This was a different world from what I was used to, but a great precursor nonetheless, helping me to survive in special forces. I tried to live a normal life in between hanging out with my friends, and being hunted by Mexican gangs for being a gringo. After a few years, something clicked inside of me. I decided not to be a victim anymore and fought back. This would have been normal for the average kid unless the student has access to firearms and decides to shoot all his or her peers at school. My induction into this particular social system, with my predisposition to be an alcoholic and with all the trauma I suffered as a child, should have been disastrous.

But I didn't get a firearm and punish innocent people; instead I learned martial arts with my criminal next-door neighbor, and I started getting a little revenge. The local gangs didn't fight as well alone and I would hunt them down one by one and beat the hell out of them. I was becoming paranoid and sneaky, and with my inhibitions lowered by alcohol, I was well on my way to being messed up early on. I wronged a few people as a teenager, for example, by robbing a few houses, broke into vehicles, and stole from the person I was babysitting for. Imagine me babysitting your kids! I even stole from my parents. But all kids do those things, right? I missed some school my junior year, and I decided it was more fun not to go. But I got my act together the next summer and went to classes to make up for lost time. I put myself back on my Ritalin, stopped drinking, and was able to graduate with my peers.

I missed out on a few key lessons though. For example, I couldn't write an essay correctly. But luckily I was always good at math. I decided I wanted to go to college with my smart friends from high school, two of which later became scientists and are making six figures today. In my infinite wisdom, I decided I wanted to be a systems engineer. I was good at math and computer programming, so why not? An already established alcoholic going to the University of Arizona—do I sense danger looming? Over the next few years, I tried to get educated but I could never quite seem to finish what I started. My drinking ramped up in Tucson, and I discovered exotic-dancer clubs. Where do you think all my money went? I learned to love kamikaze drinks though, so it was all worth it, right? I always had the intellectual capacity for what I was studying, but I just couldn't stay focused. Alcohol was already controlling my life. Every waking moment consisted of managing my life around the next drink.

I was getting myself into debt early, too, and not even getting an education to get a job to pay for it. I lived in the dormitory for a while and then moved into an apartment with my smart friends. It was great! You could see a bar from the front window, and there was a liquor store at the end of the driveway. I delivered pizzas for Godfather's Pizza in my 1972 Chevrolet Chevelle Malibu, a sweet car. I miss it. I changed my major to software engineering to lighten the workload, but it was to no avail. I drank myself into a stupor twice while living in the apartment, which set an early trend. The first time was from drinking exorbitant amounts of Southern Comfort, which seemed like a good idea at the time. The second was from chugging as many champagne bottles as humanly possible. That was just dumb. Both times, I was laid up sorry for three days, missing school. All the money I made went to my habit and not to rent or food.

The summer I went to college, I worked for a great guy in his gas station. He trusted me enough to let me close at night. I paid him back by stealing money from the small jobs I did instead of putting the money in the cash register. I also adjusted the meters at night so I could keep money. The owner was blaming the old guy, after all, the clean-cut college kid wouldn't be doing that? I bring that up because one night I drove from Tucson to Tempe in the dead of night just to break into his station and steal money. What a gem I was.

After my Godfather's pizza gig, I was hired by the campus planetarium. That was fun, educational, and lucrative, the latter especially since I wasn't putting a lot of the money for items I sold from the gift shop in the register. How the hell did I get away with all this? I have no idea, but I am pretty sure I can't use any of these employers for references! I finally gave up the idea that I was cut out to be a college boy, and I moved back in with my parents in Tempe.

I woke up one day and decided I was going to join the army reserves. I still can't remember what prompted me to do that. Much of this time was a blur. I joined up as a Forward Observer, or 13F. I basically directed artillery strikes on the battlefield for armor or infantry. I never really took basic training (BT) or advanced individual training (AIT) seriously. My peers and the drill sergeants sensed that, and everybody gave me a hard time. I suppose it wasn't cool to be a reservist in the late 1980s.

I was always getting in fights. We had open bays, and we would kick the crap out of each other, but most of it was directed at me, and I developed an early back injury from all the fights. It killed them when I got a certificate for having the highest physical fitness average. Sweet revenge! When I returned from Basic Training, my girlfriend decided she'd had enough of me, and I don't blame her. I was a mess. Besides, I didn't look very good bald, as I have quite the cone-shaped head! I am pretty sure she didn't leave me because of my goofy looking head though.

I tried to attend the DeVry Institute of Technology, but just like before, I couldn't finish what I started. I attended weekend Army Reserve training in Sierra Vista, Arizona, at Fort Huachuca, for about a year, but most of my time then was spent in Nogales, Mexico, drinking that nasty tequila with the worm. I also attended an annual exercise for two weeks in the summer, and that was enough of a delusion for me to make the next major decision in my life.

I had a few girlfriends during this time. One even gave me a venereal disease, another concrete experience to add to my list. I decided to get rid of my muscle car for a Yugo. What was I thinking? I do miss that car; I almost bought another one in 2012 off the lemon lot in Fort Bragg, North Carolina, but the wife would have killed me. I was a bit lost and without direction during this time; there was a lot of drinking and partying. I once again came up with another great idea: *I am going to go active duty and be a cool Forward Observer. I will forget about my old life, and I'll send money to my mother and let her take care of my debt.* You can do that, right? She already had her hands full with my sister, but it's still her job, right? I went down to the Phoenix Military Processing Station, or MEPS. There I found out I'd been using the wrong Social Security number for the last twenty years. What the hell! They took me anyway. I had to pay back the bonus they gave me for the Reserves, and I was in. They were sending me to Germany. I could go to another country and escape from everything. Who knew that Germany was probably the last place they should have sent an alcoholic.

CHAPTER 2

Structure

J oining up was the right thing to do, if for only getting that Social Security number fiasco figured out. I still have the wrong number on my basic training and advanced individual training certificates, but everything from this point on would be correct. The army decided to send me to Germany toward the end of December. What a gloomy place. The sun comes out maybe twice a year. I remember half of my three-year tour over there; I was drunk the other half. I was only a private and had no idea what was going on. After all, *somebody* didn't take all that army training the previous year seriously, and I had been a civilian since then.

They placed me in the barracks for the next week and had me waiting for my platoon sergeant to come pick me up. It was my first experience with "Hurry up and wait!" I did manage to find a bar with a fräulein to hang out with. And I was introduced to ouzo, and no, it doesn't contain opium.

Alcohol in Europe is a bit thicker and stronger, I soon learned. Sometime during the night I had my first, and certainly not my last, blackout experience. No, I didn't get scoped with scopolamine. I just simply drank myself into a stupor. This was one to remember. Somehow I had managed to get myself into a schoolhouse in the town and had passed out under a chalkboard. About daybreak, the janitor kicked me awake. Of course, I had no idea what the hell he was saying, but I did get his meaning. I got up and noticed I had defecated in my pants. But, having been dehydrated from the long plane ride and after all the drinking of the black, licorice-tasting liquor, I hadn't made too much of a mess! I then attempted to find my way back to the barracks. It had been dark when I arrived the night before, and now I didn't recognize anything and had no earthly idea where I was. Being lost was to become an all-too-common experience, and one that I would have to somehow get used to. Eventually, after I didn't show up for formation, the unit sent a few soldiers looking for me, but had I left anything but a good first impression. Unfortunately, that wouldn't be the last time I missed formation either and I decided to get better at drinking.

The first sergeant restricted me to the barracks until my platoon sergeant arrived, which resulted in a long awkward drive. He dropped me off in my new home, with my new roommates, who showed me around the installation. Then he took me off post to show me where all the bars were. Apparently, in all the confusion—and this was all over the holidays—the unit didn't properly process me, because a few months later my pay stopped. Somebody reported me as absent without leave, or AWOL. That was a first and last in my twenty-eight-year career.

I will never forget my roommates. We were four to a room that was twelve by twelve feet. It was a tight fit with four beds, lockers, desks, and any personal items we may have accumulated over the years. We were definitely a motley crew and all from very different backgrounds. One of my roommates would return to the States, attend and pass the Special Forces Assessment and Selection Course, or SFAS. I had no idea what any of that meant, but it sounded cool. And it would stick in my mind for another decision I would make a few years later.

Fast-forward a couple of years, and I actually ran into him in the Special Forces Qualification Course, a few classes ahead of me. He had been duped by a wily divorcee into leaving the course and had gone back to the regular Army from the special operational side, until she got what she wanted out of him and left. My other roommate was my drinking buddy, and we were affectionately referred to as the blackout twins. We would get two fifths of vodka and four bottles of orange juice from a small store outside the post and then dump out half the orange juice in each and fill them up with liquor. Why not drink the juice, you ask? "It was healthy" would be your answer. We would get two bottles for Friday night and two bottles for Saturday night. We would drink one before we left and take the other and stash it outside the club in the bushes. We would drink from that all night long, along with the local beer. We often blacked out and rolled around in the streets roughhousing.

Alcohol was plentiful and encouraged. We even had beer in the vending machine inside our barracks. A case of Budweiser on post only cost around seven dollars, too. I was in heaven. While the military did ration the liquor and cigarettes, this made the alcoholics and the smokers best friends. I joined up just as the military was doing away with allowing us to drink two beers at lunch. Bad timing. The military was starting to crack down on illegal drug use as well.

Everybody was a mess. I fit right in. One of my roommates smoked marijuana and was the local "American" dealer. I was pretty naïve about that kind of stuff, since my drug of choice was strictly alcohol. He smoked all the time, even on deployments. I remember him fashioning bongs out of soda cans in the field. We were friends, and we hung out because he was just as messed up as I was. He became the center of a big sting operation in the unit, and he ended up in chains, giving up all his local contacts. Thank God I detested smoking, as otherwise, this book would have been a bit different.

All the events with the military in Germany involved alcohol and heavy drinking, a culture I was happy to adapt to. I remember the after-party after I earned my German Armed Forces Badge of Marksmanship, or Schützenschnur, my first foreign award. There was unlimited food and as much beer and liquor as one could put down. I was a mess, and I was the bus driver.

I never learned to speak German very well because I always had people around to translate for me. I fit into the European culture and was able to get into exclusive German parties with my local friends as long as I didn't say anything. I guess the flattop blond hair, and blue eyes helped me to accomplish that. I didn't learn about cultures and start understanding them until a few years later, when I had a few Central and South America deployments under my belt. After all, it was more fun being drunk and the "Ugly American."

Sundays consisted of eating brunch on one of the air-force bases and fighting the hangover with a champagne fountain. I ended up on the rack they kept at the front gate countless times—no mattress on that sucker. After I was dropped off by the courtesy patrol—soldiers all dressed up in the business casual version in the Army with a tie collecting drunk Americans—I was picked up by my platoon sergeant the next day to sleep it off.

My sergeant even enrolled me in the Army Substance Abuse Program, or ASAP, one time after I couldn't make it to formation. They didn't care if you showed up drunk: just show up. I learned one important lesson here, and that was that I had to be careful from that point on if I was to continue drinking and not get kicked out of the military. Or else I would both begin my career in ASAP and end it there.

I wasn't a bad soldier. On the contrary, once I decided I was going to make a career out of the military, I was a great soldier. I just needed to get that first punishment out of the way. I thought I was getting out of the military, so I decided I was going to blow off the platoon sergeant and be difficult. Though painting the entire motor pool and the barracks for two weeks pretty much broke me, something changed inside, and I cannot explain it. I decided I was going to stay.

The unit I was in was getting ready to deactivate. We enjoyed long days of preparing vehicles and equipment to be placed in storage units or returned to the States. The Cold War was coming to an end. I was soon on my way to the National Training Center at Fort Irwin, California, with my first wife.

I just missed deploying to Desert Shield and Desert Storm because of the deactivation, and because I extended my tour in Germany for a year once I met my first wife. Instead, I was going to help evaluate reservist armor units prior to their deployment to the Gulf War. These were not the battle-hardened soldiers you would expect to go fight for our country. They showed up with only half their gear and no training— a bunch of sad sacks. I suppose they pawned everything, thinking they were never actually ever going to need it or be held accountable. As pathetic as the Iraqi Army was back then, these guys were worse. They didn't make the cut; instead, most of the leadership got fired.

I enjoyed interesting weather in the California desert. It even snowed in July once. Tarantulas ran amuck during their mating season. Caterpillars were everywhere once a year. Then they transformed, with their wings getting in my teeth because our cadre windshields on the Humvees didn't have glass.

You wouldn't want to give away your position to the unit being evaluated, if they saw our vehicles then they knew there was a potential enemy artillery strike. One night I drove headfirst into a big hole or tank ditch. I rang my bell on the dashboard and woke up a bit later while being pulled out of my vehicle. I had been finding locations using the odometer and the stars, good old polar navigation. In this case, I wasn't paying too much attention to what was in front of me, no lights, no night-vision device or NODs, and driving like a bat out of hell across the desert. It was the first of many head injuries I would sustain over the next twenty-eight years, which beginning in 2010 contributed to chronic headaches that haven't let up.

I didn't make much money as a sergeant, E-5. I was still in debt, married (unhappily), and given my wife's daughter, that gave us a unique set of challenges. And we were on the Women, Infants, and Children program (WIC)! My drink of choice was Jim Beam and the cheapest beer I could buy, which was Keystone, "The bottled taste in a can!" I carpooled with a buddy from Barstow, a city disguised as an oversized truck stop to Fort Irwin and back. After three days in the field, we often purchased a six-pack of Mickey's Big Mouths for the drive back home. We would be trashed by the time we got home, after so much desert dehydration. I still have drunk dreams about how good that cold beer tasted going down.

I loved computers, including building and programming them. Back then, mainframes took up entire rooms and personal computers were just starting to catch on. And I wanted a career change. I was at a point in my career where I needed to extend, reenlist, or get out. I wanted to be a computer programmer for the army. That way, I could finish my education and develop a skill that I could use on the outside as a civilian. Unfortunately for me, the reenlistment noncommissioned officer (NCO) informed me that they were reserving those positions for soldiers who were deployed to the Gulf War.

I was a bit upset—but it didn't take much to stress me out, ever. I was in the wrong place at the wrong time. The army had sent me here—why was I now being punished? I hadn't wanted to come here. If I hadn't have extended for an extra year in Germany, I would have gone to the "Big Red One" or the 1st Infantry Division and been deployed to the Gulf War.

Then I saw the bonuses on offer for joining special forces and remembered my roommate. If the army wasn't going to let me do what I wanted, then I would show them. Yes, I could still get out of this job...but I had absolutely no idea what I was getting myself into! Somebody gave me some advice about how to train up for selection, and somehow I ended up with a handbook that had an exercise program in it to get me ready. California's Fort Irwin was the perfect place to put miles on your feet, with nothing for miles but dirt roads. I had a supportive command that allowed me to train up, but I wasn't sure why. Maybe they thought it was just one of my passing fads.

I finally went to selection. The class was waiting in the old World War II barracks on the east end of Fort Bragg for everybody to show up. I linked up with a military police soldier, who I will always remember. I watched him talk himself into quitting by speculating what we were in for, before we even went out to Camp Mackall, North Carolina. I was in a combat-arms job in the army, but only armor units. I was not in the infantry. I was in for rude awakening.

I didn't have the miles on my feet with a rucksack like some of my peers, but I was smart and now I had developed the drive to finish. I had never finished anything in my life, and now it was time to make a fresh start. The army had changed me. It focused me with its structure, the same purpose for which I initially embraced the Catholic church—for the structure, but later for God, his infinite wisdom, and trusting in the path he set before me. I made it through every obstacle set before me, accomplished every task the Green Berets put in front of me successfully, and made it to the final gate. My feet were killing me, and I needed a drink.! I sat in the room with the one hundred or so candidates left, listening to the Ranger regiment soldier, who didn't think I belonged there, sitting next to me. He was making fun of me because I had my earplug case attached to my uniform pocket. Maybe I didn't belong here?

The powers that be called out the names and told them to get in formation outside. Of course, we didn't know if that was good or bad at the time. Lots of mind games were played throughout the process, all the way up until the end. Needless to say, there was tension in the room. After the last soldier filed out, they closed the door and the cadre congratulated us. Holy crap! I couldn't believe I had been selected.! They calmed us down, us down a few notches by telling us we weren't Green Berets yet, we still had long journey ahead of us. We didn't care! I was going to be a Communication Sergeant. If I made it to the end I would get a 20k bonus from the Bonus Extension and Retraining program or BEAR. I was also told I was going to 10th Special Forces Group (A) but that changed to 7th Special Forces Group (A) later. God was guiding me. He wanted me to meet my soul mate. By this time my first wife was pregnant with my son. I had to report to Fort Benning, GA for airborne training because I was a "dirty red leg," a term used by airborne Soldiers to describe non-airborne and artillery. I dropped my wife and her daughter with my parents and departed for school. I am pretty sure she never forgave me for that. My first marriage was never meant to be, I know that now. I am going to blame myself. We both had our faults but we weren't compatible. She hated the military life and Special Forces, it was a joke to her, but it was my world now. She also hated my family. I don't think we actually had anything in common and we quickly grew apart. I was just a dumb enlisted Soldier bringing home an exotic woman from a different land! The drinking was curbed during the next year, only on weekends for the most part. I took a break from the qualification course when my son was born. The drinking ramped up during that time. I was drunk when he was born on Fort Bragg. I drove my wife to the hospital in that state and it wouldn't be the last time.

I learned Morse code, special ops communications, small unit tactics, unconventional warfare, and finished with Spanish. All within 18 months or so. It was a long journey but anti-climatic, something was missing, or maybe I was having glimpses of my eventual collapse. I still didn't know what I was getting myself into. I graduated donned my beret and was officially a Special Forces Communications Sergeant in 1993. I wasn't happy, giving in to the bottle and work were my only solace. I reported in to 7th Special Forces Group and was assigned to 3rd Battalion and got on with the next chapter in my life.

CHAPTER 3
Golden Years

was in the best physical shape of my life. Yes, always drinking to get drunk but getting right up the next morning and running it completely out of my system. Oh, to be young again. Nobody ever mentioned that I smelled like a brewery. As a team guy, that was acceptable, as long as you didn't get in an accident or get arrested. The longer we visited the desert, the more incidents our community would accumulate. Later on, as a sergeant major, I had to be careful, and my wife was very helpful as my enabler. Life on a Special Forces Operational Detachment Alpha, or SFODA, was good. It was my family, and it always came first.

I have done some questionable and stupid things over the years, but the alcohol was in control. At first, I didn't realize it. Then time passed and it did start worrying me; eventually it had its claws dug deep and I didn't care anymore. I didn't care whether it was slowly killing me or who I was hurting, but that is for a later chapter.

I was a cocky buck sergeant, and I knew everything. All you had to do was ask me. As a good friend once told me, "Sergeant first classes or E-7s are the smartest guys in special forces, just ask one!" Luckily, by the time I made it to that rank I was humbled a bit, and I didn't act too much like a knucklehead. My first deployment was to a remote location in the Peruvian jungle, where the only way in was by boat or plane. At the time, it was a neutral zone for all the drug runners and insurgents to go take a "time out" from all the illegal activities. They even respected each other there, so there were no skirmishes except for the occasional drunken brawl. It was hot, what we like to call "a thousand degrees of hell," and the entire town took a siesta every day from 1:00 p.m. to 3:00 p.m. It was just enough time to get over your morning drunk and start your early afternoon drinking binge. Once again, it was a terrible place for an alcoholic to be hanging out.! These days it is buzzing with tourists and casinos with a fancy concrete boardwalk along the Amazon River, and it is actually a very relaxing place to visit if you don't mind the mosquitoes. My SFODA was supporting the host nation by monitoring an air bridge that differentiated between authorized aircraft flights and drug runners. It took the military a few years to get the procedures correct; the government even put a few holes in a Hercules C-130. Shooting down first *is* a technique, just not the appropriate one, especially when innocent lives are involved. The mission was shut down in my area, and we got a few months of down time, waiting for a decision on whether to continue the project or pull out.

I was happy, though. I had learned my communication craft, and there was plenty of adventure to be had. However, an alcoholic, asshole gringo, running amuck in a remote town in Peru—that was not a good combination. I hadn't learned what being a special forces soldier was all about yet. I pissed off more locals than befriending them, but this would all change, and I eventually developed some lifelong friendships. I was allowed to make mistakes, I came out of that deployment understanding what I had gotten myself into career-wise, and I liked it.

This deployment was an adventure, and it spoiled me. The next one would not be so cozy. I drank as if it was going out of style, and my alcohol tolerance was improving. I installed a solar-power charger on a friend's boat; he worked for a three-letter organization. As a reward, he let me borrow it, along with his driver, and tour the Amazon a bit. The Amazon is a beautiful place, with its pink dolphins, gigantic catfish, piranhas, and, of course, the ever-annoying mosquitoes that carried a myriad of fun diseases. Good times.

I did develop some bad habits during that deployment, one of which was wandering off alone to the shady part of town to sit on the plastic chairs, hang out, and drink with the locals. This habit would come back to bite me in the rear in a future deployment. I went about as native as a gringo could go, given the amount of time I spent there. I didn't want to leave.! I stayed sick the entire deployment, and I don't think I had a solid stool the entire time. I even contracted dengue fever, a nasty, mosquito-borne disease. The onset of the fever hit me as I was driving another gentleman to the airport. I almost drove us off the road, and he had to take me back to the hotel. I don't remember much of the next two weeks, except that it sucked. I am pretty sure that I contracted every ailment a gringo could possibly get, and only survived because my blood was always thinned out with alcohol and I ate plenty of spices. I didn't get sick on any future deployments, however, except for a mysterious illness I still get once a year. In that case, the army tried to figure out what it was, couldn't, and gave up. That was our culture—thin medical records combined with several undocumented medical problems at the end of our careers. I managed to contract dengue fever again in the Philippines. I was told there are five strains, and that one of them will kill you. The others you can only contract once. I was now two of five on the revolver!

I went from a deployment where I was the only gringo of three Green Berets and on my own, to a battalion deployment, living in tents and washing in water buffaloes and waterfalls. Don't get me wrong; it was still an adventure, just a little more structured. Back then, we received large amounts of cash, which we carried to pay for food, rentals, lodging, and an operational fund covering any unforeseen costs. However, on this deployment, I thought I was making $44 per day; instead, I was merely making $3.50, to help with incidentals. At least that's what the army calls it. Even though I don't recall anybody saying we weren't supposed to get all that cash, six months' worth, the army is always right, and the situation would come back to bite me in the butt at the end of this deployment.

The mission was called Operation Safe Border, and it took place in the mid-1990s. The Peruvian and Ecuadorian governments and populations hated each other, with disputes originating over land rights. We were there, along with representatives from Argentina, Chile, and Brazil—which I liked to call the ABCs—to disarm both sides. An officer from each country participated, along with a US Special Forces pair consisting of an officer and a commo guy, which was me. We flew out to remote locations between each country's border in a US Blackhawk, which had the fuel pods painted white so neither side would shoot us down. They would still target us, though, causing aircraft-warning lights to flash and the pilots to fly at treetop level. We would watch them disarm and send reports back to our base of operation, which we called Higginsville, named after our battalion commander. We loved that guy. I would run into him again as a team sergeant and as a company sergeant major in Colombia, where he was working as a civilian overseeing the progress of the forces we were training. I will never forget the vampire bats infesting the camps in the outposts of the lower jungles on the Peruvian side. Those little suckers, a small joke, could really move on the ground. They low-crawled on their small wing joints, and they looked like little black mice scuttling along on the ground. We all had to weigh down the bottom portions of our mosquito nets because the bats would low-crawl underneath them, climb up on you, bite you while numbing the spot with their saliva, and suck your blood.! They also had rabies, which was bad for the South American soldiers. The health care was bad enough in the big cities, but anything contracted in the jungle was fatal. They would hunt them down during the day and kill them, exacting their revenge on them for their fallen comrades by injecting syringes full of water into them until they burst. It was messy but it made the Peruvian Soldiers feel better and entertained me! If the Soldiers weren't killed by the myriad of unaccounted land mines that were strewn everywhere the bats would get them. That was a future mission developing for Special Operations, the munitions and land mines were scattered throughout the jungles on both sides and the jungle grows fast, also ammunition would wash up along the shores all along the river, not a good thing for a small child to find. It was a hazard for the local populace that lived out there, and there were plenty that did. Halfway through the deployment we were allowed to pick a designated location to take a break, I chose Panama. I stayed in the Army barracks there on the Pacific side and proceeded to spend well over $1500 in a week. I wish I had known that wasn't my money at the time, as I might have curbed the partying a bit. As it turned out, I had to get a civilian loan to pay back the government.

My first of six deployments to Colombia was to a remote location outside a small town called Cimitarra, which is in the Santander Department in the northeastern part of the country. We had to transfer our gear via a Russian helicopter—it was either an Mi-8 or Mi-17—because the roads were too dangerous to travel. We flew out of the city of Bucaramanga. I always loved that name, and the name Tortuga, or turtle!

The Colombian officer in charge of our training outpost was a bit eccentric. We always worked hard and played hard, but he took play hard to a new level. He would fly in cases of Chivas Regal for his weekend-long parties. My team leader and team sergeant were stuck there and, although the Colombian officer expected the rest of us to participate, he understood we had to prepare for the following week's training.

The parties lasted from Friday, after the day's work was done, into late Sunday night or early Monday morning. That guy could drink. He would make us learn to dance with the other officers' wives, which was awkward. We would sneak out sometimes, and go down to the town outside of the outpost. But if we stayed out too long, he would send his soldiers in jeeps to round us up. He knew he was responsible for a bunch of gringos in a bad area.

There were members of the Revolutionary Armed Forces of Colombia (FARC) who hung out in one of the local bars in the town. They weren't shy to let us know that either. They seemed friendly enough, buying us drinks and showing us their ID cards. They must have been up in their ranks, too, because they had several vehicles and armed guards. They spoke some English, and my buddy and I spent some time with them. I was separated from him several hours later, ending up in the home of one of the locals, getting even drunker. Then the local disappeared, leaving me alone. I was drunk, but I sensed something was wrong. I started seeing several individuals looking in from the high, open windows lining all the rooms, a common part of the architecture throughout Central and South America. They spotted me, and the door suddenly was kicked in. Simultaneously—and my recollection is hazy—I prepared to defend myself. But one of my senior special forces compadres showed up outside, with several jeeps with a squad of armed Colombian soldiers, and got me out of there. I will always be grateful to him and to God for keeping me safe that day. Of course, I got my scolding from him all the way to the outpost. But I learned a valuable, concrete lesson about the buddy system then, and I would never repeat my actions. Who knows, I might have ended up getting really immersed in the culture and, after being rescue d, receiving a Harley Davidson (like some folks were about to get many years later from their captivity). Or not!

I did actually go on one noncombat deployment and not drink. I was in El Salvador, and I can't even remember why I didn't drink, but my recalcitrance only lasted until the end of the deployment. That was an exciting trip. I conducted my first jump. I was a fresh, new jumpmaster in a joint operation with the host nation, jumping out of an old C-26 airplane. I remember that because we had to extend the static lines, since the cable that they attached to was on the opposite side of the door. This was also the trip where I developed my arachnophobia, maybe in part because I was detoxing from alcohol. We jumped in with our counterparts for a field exercise we were running, conducting light infantry patrols for about one week. We conducted patrol base operations during the day and ran patrols throughout the night. I was following one such patrol on a moonless night through the jungle. The Soldiers were shorter than I was and were able to traverse the obstacles a lot better. They missed all the spider webs, but I didn't, and after the fifth one crawled down my back, I freaked out, turned on my trusty G-Shock watch super-light, beat brush to a clearing, and began stripping to get all the creepy crawlies off of me! Not a good night, but it entertained the hell out of my teammates and the locals. I would have nightmares about spiders for the next couple of years, some pre-PTSD.

During this period I married my beautiful (and current) wife, who is from Peru. For the next three years, we partied pretty hard at home and at clubs. We decided to have a baby, but even that didn't convince me to slow down or stop drinking. Unlike during my first marriage, I did actually want to go home after work, but I still couldn't stop drinking. My wife only knew me as an alcoholic, but somehow she saw past all that and stuck with me anyway. I was in the Special Warfare Training Group (A), or SWTG (A), during our pregnancy with our daughter. I would take her with me out to Camp Mackall, North Carolina so I could keep an eye on her in case she went into labor, while I watched the students at night. I wish she had gone into labor then, because I would have been sober at the hospital. As it was, at home I couldn't curb the drinking even when she was dilated. This would be the second time I would watch with a hangover as one of my children was being born. I love my children more than life itself. I am so happy to be sober today, so I can be there as a Dad and not as a drunk.

I became a team sergeant or master sergeant, E-8, in 2003. I deployed to Colombia again and worked with the national police at their training academy. I continued to drink, but as long as I took care of the guys and the mission was accomplished, it was OK, right? I had been to this country several times before, as a team guy, and had built up some contacts in the government, the military, local law enforcement, and several three-letter agencies, which now had old-timer seventh Groupers working there. I didn't need them yet, but I would in the future as advanced operations base (AOB) sergeant major. Our battalion was the last to get into the Seventh SFG (A) rotation into Afghanistan. My SFODA was one of the two that would integrate into the combat rotation. My team leader and warrant officer went on to bigger and better things, so I commanded the SFODA for that rotation until we returned. My guys decided to purchase a kegerator when we returned for the team room, which is not recommended when the team sergeant is an alcoholic. We would fill up our Nalgene bottles and drink during team meetings at the end of the day. Our days would end earlier and earlier.!

I transitioned into the Headquarters and Headquarters Company, or HHC, as first sergeant, or 1SG, in 2006. It was just in time, too, because my wife was getting tired of picking me up drunk from the company or the Green Beret club.

I sobered up and stayed that way for the most part during my short time at Fort Bragg. I couldn't conduct any 1SG business smelling like alcohol. I witnessed some both entertaining and horrendous things that humans can do to other humans, even their children. It was the kind of stuff that wasn't supposed to happen here in the States. I was wrong. Sometimes the government and myriad redundant social systems can overlook the obvious, yet let monsters walk away free because of stereotyping trumping proper investigations.

I soon deployed again to Afghanistan, this time as a 1SG. I was always lucky to have great officers to work with in special forces. They were all great men and even better soldiers. The HHC commander was one of the best. I found out toward the end of that rotation that I had been picked for promotion to sergeant major, or E-9, in the secondary zone.

I was further promoted to sergeant first class, or E-7, at my second look in the primary zone, and then to master sergeant, or E-8, at my first look in the primary zone. Being picked up for sergeant major got me caught up with my peers. I would only be an acting command sergeant major at battalion and group level, but I would never see the rank. And it is a good thing I didn't. God had other plans for me, and it didn't involve the military. Instead, it involved recovery and salvation.

CHAPTER 4

Turning My Back on God

eavy drinking eventually takes its toll, mentally, physically, and spiritually. I would like to think I was a great special forces leader whom other people would want to emulate. I would like to think I always did the right thing, put the mission first, but first and foremost took care of soldiers. I could have been so much more, but the bottle controlled me: a better father, a better husband, a better soldier. But I couldn't stop. Lord knows I tried over the years. I was finally able to stop before a long combat deployment, only because I knew I was going to continue drinking the moment it was over. For many of us, the first couple of weeks always become the detox period. Instead of keeping up with current events with my community, I isolated myself and focused only on the moment. I was very good at hiding my problems. Only the people closest to me knew just how bad my drinking problem was.

After I handed over the company and my diamond, this is a leadership position in the entire military and is designated with a symbol of a diamond within the rank, to one of my peers, I moved back to Third Battalion, Seventh Special Forces Group Airborne, which is where I originally started. Here I worked operations and was the acting command sergeant major, or CSM, until the actual major arrived from his previous tour. I was in a holding pattern, waiting to go to the United States Army Sergeants Major Academy (USASMA). I soon got my first taste of what I was going to be going through soon as rear detachment group operations sergeant major, a year or so later, working tasks for funeral details. These were for soldiers I didn't know, mostly retired, but there would soon be a flood of those I did know personally. I pinned my star on here, my last rank insignia. I was a special forces sergeant major, a major accomplishment. I had come a long way from my days in Europe.

It was time to depart for USASMA at Fort Bliss, Texas. The post was ten minutes from the Mexico border. Trucks were being stolen and driven across the border like it was going out of style. The following year was a miserable one for me and especially for my family. It should have been a time for us to get closer and enjoy ourselves, especially since I was getting a break from the constant deployments. My son came to live with us. His mother didn't want to deal with him, but I wouldn't find out the whole truth until a few years later. I am not even sure if knowing would have changed anything, I would like to think I would have gotten him help instead of making things worse. He was starting high school and my daughter was in elementary school. Her school was a few blocks from where we lived on post.

I was a drunk, and I had plenty of time to feed the habit. There was some serious multitasking going on, which I was always good at. I would get up early in the morning to run the alcohol out of my system. Then I'd get my son up to do his chores, which usually involved my blood pressure elevating. I definitely had anger issues. I would walk my daughter to school, and then meet up with the bike-riding gang to go to class at the academy, to learn how the army wanted me to think. I would return home, work on my college homework, pick up my daughter from school, meet my son at the door, get pissed at him for something, and then take him on a long counseling run up and down a very steep mountain road. I would end the day by drinking until I passed out. I would get up the next day, repeat, and rinse.

Everybody always saw us as a happy, well-adjusted family and always thought that we had a perfect marriage. The wife and I were very good at hiding it. I still meet people today that are surprised that I am an alcoholic. My son wasn't doing well in school. He could have been a straight-A student if he had just applied himself, none of which was his fault. He brought some serious baggage with him, just like his old man. I was so blinded by rage that I couldn't think straight. Any rational person would have realized that something was wrong. "" Tension was in the air every day in our home, and I stayed pissed off for ten months. I wasn't deployed, but my family wished I was. They suffered; it was a bad time for all of us.

Even though I treated my son like crap, and I still haven't forgiven myself for the things I did, he did become quite the cardio animal from our numerous counseling runs. He lettered his freshman year in wrestling, which was his stepping stone to a career in mixed martial arts. A few years later, I was so happy that he still wanted to talk to me. He told me that he wanted to learn how to defend himself. I am not going to go into any more detail on that subject except to mention that his mother knew why.

The only reason I didn't have an aneurism, a heart attack, liver failure, or alcohol poisoning was because of all the running I did. It was a stress reliever for me. Doctors today are still impressed with my liver's resiliency; many people are less fortunate. All the drinking, stress, and anger did give me excruciatingly painful acid reflux. That all started in 1998. I have had several endoscopies and colonoscopies over the years. I had three colonoscopies before I even turned fifty.

I honestly can't remember my family being happy, or even feeling safe from me, during that time. I was such a crappy father and husband. My wife would take my daughter with her to Peru, and she actually contemplated not coming back or leaving me when she returned. And I wouldn't have blamed her if she did. I have no memories of anybody smiling during that turbulent time. My wife was an enabler and had to shield my daughter from me later on. She was already very good at hiding it from my workplace and from our friends. I never laid a hand on either of them, but my outbursts terrified them and would often end with me striking a wall or throwing something.

My fellow Green Berets were either living on post in the same military housing area or out in the economy. We partied every weekend. There were unending reasons to drink, whether it was football, NASCAR, kids' parties—or, hell, who needs a reason to drink! We always had plenty of alcohol in our homes and, if we ran out, there was a store right down the street, within walking distance. We eventually got our new assignments. Originally, I was supposed to be in charge of our commando school in Afghanistan; instead, that changed to Rear Detachment group operations sergeant major. I would be overseeing all operations we conducted all over the world, and the deaths associated with them.

My son returned to his mother, not any better off than when he left. I am sure she blames me for everything, but it takes two to tango. The rest of us started our journey back to Fort Bragg. I was able to get on-post housing immediately, a nice perk for being a sergeant major. My wife departed for Peru with my daughter, and I had to fend for myself for three weeks. I began working right away, but was to spend much more time with the deputy commanding officer (DCO) instead of the group operations officer, performing duties above my position. I had to wait one combat rotation before I would be able to take over my company, our next command position after team sergeant. I was drinking every night, and I found out just how dependent I was on my wife for everything.!

The combat deaths starting happening two weeks after I started. I always hated referring to friends and service members as Killed in Action (KIA) or Wounded in Action (WIA), but you had to try to dehumanize the process or you would never get through it. I still feel guilty, since I wasn't over there with the group, but I understood the importance of what I was doing. I was miserable, the academy was a stressful time, and now I was home alone.

An alcoholic does what an alcoholic does best when alone; drink until passing out. I wasn't any different. I wasn't even eating. I would get the phone call between one and three o'clock in the morning that one of ours had fallen. I would still be drunk when I got dressed and drove to work to start the process. We had a working relationship with Fort Bragg Mortuary Affairs, who would send us the official message and let us handle it from there. They were then happy to stand aside, as they were busy enough.

I would already be in the basement of group headquarters, filling out the board and preparing to brief the staff. The notification and casualty assistant Teams all came from within our unit. We took care of our own in special forces; our family encompassed the soldiers' families. I think back on those times, each time showing up in the middle of the night smelling like alcohol. Nobody ever said anything about it, I suppose either because I got the job done or because I was a sergeant major. I was always taking care of soldiers, and sergeant majors are immortal and never have problems.

Who looks out for us? I set up and participated in every unit memorial service for each and every soldier, all the way up to the last one. God was looking out for me because I couldn't do one more. I attended every wake and funeral service conducted by the families. I traveled all over the country with the DCO, consoling the families and helping where I could. We would help at the family funeral service when requested to do so, by providing pallbearers, ushers, a bugler, firing detail, and a bagpipe player, and worked with the general officer who presented the flag to the family. I did this over and over during 2008, but it was a bad rotation for our group. I couldn't take it anymore.

My life at home was a blur from the alcohol use. I was there, but I really wasn't there. My wife had to take care of everything, and she was always walking on eggshells around me. The littlest thing would set me off. I couldn't sleep at night without drinking; I even started hearing things and hallucinating. I turned my back on God. With all the death I was dealing with, I couldn't bring myself to go to church or even to have God in my thoughts. I even tried to call out to friends for help, especially the one that brought me into the church. I was spiritually sick. I would find out, however, that although I turned my back on God, he didn't turn his back on me. He would soon intervene in my life because he had other plans for me.

I finally moved down to First Battalion where I would take my company, but I wasn't free yet. The group operations officer took a company at the same time. The Group wanted us to return and guide the new staff through the casualty process. Then the battalion wanted us to assist them. The only solace I found was my deployments to Central and South America. I would soon be cashing in all my favors in the next two deployments to Colombia. I will not go into detail, but it is safe to say that with all my contacts I saved a few careers. It was all part of God's plan and the path he had set before me. As a drunk, with chronic headaches, depression, and anger and anxiety issues, with a chip on my shoulder, I wasn't ready to forgive anybody, warranted or not. I was surviving by running thirty miles a week and numbing my problems every chance I could get. The running was about to become harder, but the drinking didn't stop; it only escalated.

My next job was in late 2010, working as the operations sergeant major in the Special Warfare Training Group Airborne (SWTG (A)). This is when the headaches became unbearable. The only relief I could get was from Percocet or alcohol. The Percocet was killing me with constipation, and it was addicting and in short supply, so I weaned myself off it and drank more instead. The army put me through hundreds of different tests, trying to figure out what was wrong with me. It was debilitating at times and was starting to affect adversely my job performance.

The guys gave me a plaque on the way out that read, "Thank you for your Professionalism, Mentorship, Direction, and Hard Work. (When you weren't in the hospital)!" I also developed some stomach issues, problems with fevers again, and along with the alcohol, they were starting to adversely affect my running. If I couldn't run, I would not be able to heal my body. I was passing out at home after runs and was losing two to three pounds per week. I looked and felt like I was wasting away. I was worse off than I would have been at Ranger school, before women attended, or at a Survival, Evasion, and Resistance and Escape (SERE) course. I started coughing up blood and had it in my stool. What the hell was going on?

I moved within the organization to be the sergeant major of the Special Warfare Education Group Airborne (SWEG (A)). This would be the closest I would get to being a command sergeant major. My problems persisted, and I started seeing and hearing things in my home. The wife and I thought that maybe the place was haunted, so we placed crucifixes all over the place. The hair would stand up on the back of my neck every time I passed our bedroom closet. I had childhood fears of the boogeyman in there, especially after I read the short story "The Boogeyman," written by Stephen King. I was a big, bad Green Beret afraid of the closet! Of course, none of this stuff was really happening. My mind, body, and spirit were weak and clouded.

Even given these problems, I was still restless. I hadn't deployed for two years. I always seem to find myself in the wrong place at the wrong time for rotations into the desert, or was that circumstance intentional? I had only had two under my belt. The last one didn't fall into that category.

The Group CSM decided after the academy that I was a better fit burying our fallen comrades than deploying. The United States Army John F. Kennedy Special Warfare Center and School (USAJFKSWCS) CSM was a good man, and he was going to work with me and our higher-ups to get me deployed. Although I knew he wouldn't have sent me if he knew half the stuff that was going on with me, luckily nobody talked about my illnesses. He passed on the request for my deployment to the United States Army Special Operations Command (USASOC) CSM. He was also my group CSM and team sergeant. Everybody changes over the years, for good, bad, or indifferent. The deployment location changed three times, but I didn't mind because I was deploying! The final location was to be the Philippines. I would have preferred Afghanistan, but it was still considered a combat deployment and I hadn't done that as a sergeant major. I went to see him to get my instructions and maybe reminisce about the old days, and I slipped up and mentioned that I'd had some problems with weight loss. He was a bit angry, but I was able to assure him that I was good to go, even though I wasn't. I thought I needed to deploy, I was going to be on my way to the Philippines, a part of the world reserved for First Special Forces Group Airborne, for a year. Boy, was that a mistake.

CHAPTER 5

End of an Era

The trip to Texas put a strain on my marriage, which is funny if you think about it. What didn't put a strain on it? And marriages are work, right? Afterwards, I got to spend two weeks in Hawaii. It should have been a vacation, but I hate the water. I would rather have spent my off time in the hotel drinking, anyway. I wasn't complaining, though, because I was actually deployed. I eventually made it to the capital city of Manila in the Philippines, and I immediately learned that the Embassy Suites had unlimited free alcohol from 5:00 p.m. to 8:00 p.m. every night. I was in heaven. I didn't spend a lot of time there, but I did have business at the Embassy Suites once or twice a month. Otherwise, I would be on the southernmost portion of the continent, which consisted of about seven thousand or so islands. Crazy, right? I had been trained to operate in Central and South America, but the culture in the Philippines really wasn't that much different. There were jungles and Spanish influences, especially in the town of Zamboanga City, where I would be spending most of my time.

I did make my mark there on the Philippine compound. We had a small temporary compound within their base. There was family housing and a small shop right behind us. There was a rotting boardwalk and a platform standing in front of the shop to keep people out of the water when it rained, and it did all the time.! I would go down there to visit, and I would fall through the wood slats. It was in bad shape. I decided to build a gazebo using my own money. The locals did an excellent job, and I now had a place to hide. They even put a nice plaque inside, thanking me.

I always accomplished what I was sent to do, no matter what the job or task. Here, I was given detailed directives by my boss at USASOC, and I accomplished them. That had never been hard for me. I had always been able to focus on the moment. But it was getting harder. While the headaches weren't getting any better, I was learning to cope with them. This would all change in two years. It would soon come to a blistering head, and I would come crashing down hard. Also, I met a lifelong friend in the Philippines. He was the post CSM for Western Mindanao command. The culture was both similar to what I was used to and different. The language was a mixture of Tagalog, Spanish, and English. After listening, I was able to pick up enough content to understand what they were talking about. Even though I would switch to full-on Spanish the drunker I got. They didn't understand that! He was a drinker and had a good grasp of English, so we immediately connected. He would take me all over town and even on some island-hopping adventures.

Whenever one of us sergeant majors experiences a change of heart about a job and decides to retire, there is an avalanche of change. My bosses would spend weeks trying to figure out where we were all going, but nothing was ever set in stone. I was supposed to spend one year in this position, but I would be yanked out to take my next job, which would be my last one as well.

God continued to take care of me by manipulating those around me, to keep me on my path. He definitely works in mysterious ways. I returned stateside and, as I would soon find out, for a very good reason. My daughter was diagnosed with Ehlers-Danlos syndrome (EDS) and infantile scoliosis at a very young age. Though scoliosis is a fairly common condition, and our physicians have come a long way from the "Forest Gump" days, her EDS caused complications.

She had worn a brace since she was three years old, and the curvature of her spine had been stabilized for many years. But when I returned from the Philippines and we all went to our six month follow-up at Chapel Hill, what we were told shocked us and scared the hell out of my wife and daughter. The curvature was now well beyond the point where she needed surgery, and she was only twelve years old. I let my boss know, and he allowed me to put my next job on hold until my daughter was taken care of. I continued to drink, though, and it escalated now that I didn't have anybody to report to in person. That was not a good thing. My health was getting steadily worse. The hospital visits were becoming more frequent. My blood was always drenched with alcohol and I had no clue if it caused by that or past problems or injuries. That was something I wouldn't be able to differentiate until I detoxed and learned to cope with my addiction. I had blood in my stool again, too, so I was off to get another colonoscopy. And by the way, since I was there, they would throw in an endoscopy to check my acid reflux problem. The headaches were happening daily now, and every little thing would set me off. I remember falling down the stairs in my on-post housing at Fort Bragg. Being drunk helped me to avoid injuries; at least that's what I thought at the time.

It was finally time to take my daughter to the hospital for her surgery. I couldn't even stop drinking long enough to take her there sober. I can only say that God had to have had other plans for me. I still thank him to this day that I didn't hurt or kill my family, innocent bystanders, or myself in a car accident. We were able to stay in her room while she was recovering. I needed to be strong, but I was helpless. I couldn't take her pain away, though I would have switched places with her in a second. She will have chronic pain in her back for the rest of her life because of the EDS. We brought her home, and we did everything we could for her. It was getting harder for us to cope with life, because my wife was falling deeper and deeper into depression and I was getting increasingly useless at home because of the drinking.

A few months later, I had to move on to my last job in the army. The move to Virginia was a culture shock to me. The traffic was horrendous, and the people definitely didn't have the same temperament as Carolinians. The home we found was only five miles from Fort Belvoir, Virginia. There was a supermarket within walking distance of our townhouse and a liquor store inside the gas station right outside the compound where I worked. Everything was setting me up for disaster. The work hours were based on travel times, so the building would clear out except for a few individuals. I started out being one of those but, as time went on, I spent less and less time at work. I never thought about how much I was drinking. I was functioning well enough for the first six months. My enemy was in complete control of me and my body held up exceptionally well, but it was catching up with me.

I was helping the unit and still taking care of service members. The organization was going through some changes, and I was able to offer my help from the curriculum experience I learned in USAJFKSWCS. The unit knowledge was extensive and very important to our nation's safety. The problem was that it was being passed on from individual to individual, without much of it written down. If everyone was changed out all at once, the mission would be degraded. I would like to think I was able to help the unit before I fell. My life was my job. Today, I know that shouldn't have been my focus, and it isn't anymore.

I couldn't put 100 percent of my effort into my job or my life anymore, because my every waking moment revolved around getting my next drink. What made me such a great soldier before now made me a great drunk. If I went out to dinner with my family, we had to eat right as the restaurant opened. I would be calculating in my head how much time I would have to drink when I returned home before eventually going to bed. I would always set a time to stop drinking, but I never followed it, and eventually I had to go to work later and later or not at all. I never saw a movie in the evening. I might see the first or second showing on a weekend, but never on a weekday.

I thought I was happy, but I wasn't. I loved my family, but I wasn't there for them. I was always stressed. If the day went long and it cut my drinking short, I would be agitated and take it out on those around me. Nobody at work had a clue about the extent and seriousness of my drinking, and I never drank there after-hours. I was a solitary alcoholic. I remember going to a Washington Nationals game with the guys from work. It was raining and cold. I made it to the bar with one of my buddies. I had a few there and started getting a good buzz going. When the rain let up, we made it to our seats. They were nice, on the front row at the third base side. I proceeded to buy drinks for myself and everybody sitting around me. We had a mess there with all the empty aluminum bottles. I must have spent well over $700 at the game. And I was drunk by the time game was over, but instead of going home I went to an outside bar and continued to drink. I was too drunk to make my way home. There were three metro train changes and a cab ride at the end of that. I would have slept out somewhere if one of my navy buddies hadn't escorted me all the way to the taxi.

But my friends didn't think anything of it; they just thought the sergeant major was having a good time. It was a common practice for me. I drank to get drunk, and it didn't matter if I was at a friend's house or a military ball. I went to the Mall in Washington, DC, for the Fourth of July celebration. We were on the lawn behind the Washington Monument. We stayed in a hotel with another family of friends, so we didn't have to drive home that night. They brought beer, but it wasn't enough. We were on the lawn just after lunchtime. We ran out of beer fast, and I needed a lot more than they brought. I couldn't buy enough from the vendors because the lines were out of control, and the lines to the urinals were even worse. I was in a living nightmare. I couldn't wait to get out of there and to the hotel. It was probably one of the best fireworks shows anywhere, second only to Disney World, and I wasn't enjoying it. I was agitated to say the least. I was finally able to drink my fill in the hotel restaurant. My wife was always so embarrassed for me throughout the years, As I always drank too much at parties or events. I always started too early and passed out too early.

Going back, when I was promoted to sergeant major I threw a party at the Green Beret club at Fort Bragg. When you were promoted, it was an expectation that you spend the monetary difference on the party between your old salary and the new, which was considerable. I did my best to get as many pitchers possible. I got so drunk that my buddies had to put me in my car. When we got home, my wife had to get a neighbor to help carry me to bed.

After I finished my company sergeant major tour, I threw a going-away party for the guys. My wife wasn't there for that one. When she came to pick me up at the Green Beret club, it was closed and we were gone. I wasn't there because we had continued the party in downtown Fayetteville. Eventually, the headquarters and support company first sergeant, a Green Beret, and my sober designated driver, drove me home along with my favorite team sergeant and team leader. They were both from the Military Freefall Team. Both of them were great soldiers and they both made sergeant major themselves. They dropped me off on my lawn with my wife yelling, and I got out of there to safety.! The story sounds funny, but my wife put up with a lot of crap from me over the years.

I always loved her and I still do today. I wouldn't be alive today if it wasn't for her. She took care of me as my wife and my enabler. She loved me and always put me and my career first, before herself. I didn't deserve it. I am so glad to have her in my life. Any lesser woman would have left me. I was wearing her out though—all those nights of listening to me, making sure I didn't stop breathing from alcohol poisoning. I was destroying her. All I could think about was when I was going to get drunk again, and I couldn't even see what I was doing to her.

I lived for hangovers. My doctors always get a kick out of that when I tell them. It focused me. I never needed a drink to get me going in the morning. The hangover sufficed. That strange relationship between the bottle the night before and the hangover throughout the day allowed me to survive as long as I did in the service. The end of an era was coming, however. God was guiding me to a point of no return. Then it happened.

CHAPTER 6

Rock Bottom

didn't know it but, I was being led to this point in my life. Even if you don't believe in God, in reading this chapter you won't be able to deny that something intervened. I hadn't had any higher power in my life for some time. I had turned my back on him, and I was spiritually weak Luckily, he hadn't turned his back on me. I didn't know it, but I had been in a holding pattern to take a battalion as a command sergeant major. The job didn't provide a pay raise, just a lot more headaches. I don't know why I was so stuck on getting this position. I'd had an excellent career, even with the baggage I carried through all those years. Not many soldiers make sergeant major in the conventional army, so to make it in special forces is quite an accomplishment. I suppose it was my competitive nature, or maybe just boredom; after all, I had been in this rank for eight years. It was never meant to be, though, and if I had taken the position, I would have gotten divorced and possibly drank myself to death.

I had decided my unit needed a coin that better represented what we did. This is a common object used by units throughout the Armed Forces for Esprit de Corp. The problem was that the only authorized coin was at the highest level. None of which made any sense, because civilian leadership only dealt with politics and the rest of the unit actually worked real-world missions. I was in one of two small contingents primarily made up of special operations, and I was the Senior Enlisted Advisor (SEA) for these folks. The worst part of the situation is that the civilian leadership made it almost impossible to get their coins because little old ladies in white tennis shoes decided who actually warranted receiving them. Not that anybody we worked with actually wanted one—but that's not the point! This organization was joint, meaning it had officers and enlisted folks from each of the armed forces, but it was run by civilians. We were there to advise them, but we had all the cool gadgets and toys, so they used and abused us during every Very Important Person (VIP) visit. The worst part is that they didn't empower any noncommissioned officers anywhere in the organization. It was poorly run, and if I had been in a better state of mind, I would have championed getting us the hell out of there and embedding that skill within all SOF units. It was the standard government agency, poorly run, with too many redundant positions and systems. A cleansing needs to take place within the government, reducing government employees in all levels by substantial numbers instead of downsizing the much-needed military.

Anyway, I decided I would raffle off some items to raise money to pay for these coins. One such item was an antique shotgun I inherited from my grandfather. An important piece of information to point out here is that the shotgun still had a round lodged in it. I had flown from Arizona to North Carolina with several weapons, and I don't know why I didn't clear them all. I was grieving with the passing of my grandfather, and I guess you can say I wasn't thinking straight. I brought them home and put them in the gun safe. They had moved a few times with me until the day I took this particular piece to work.

I was so programmed by the army and special forces that I should have known better. I had fired all my weapons at one time or another. The one exception was this weapon. I don't engage in "what if it" anymore; this was meant to be. It was the first of several concrete experiences I would encounter that would lead to my eventual breakdown and recovery. I brought the shotgun to post and right into my workplace. This is something I did it all the time at Fort Bragg, into my team room, but I was soon to find out it was frowned upon at Fort Belvoir, Virginia.

I showed the gun to one the retired contractors, a lieutenant colonel in special forces, who was also an avid hunter and gun collector. I wanted him to appraise it. I needed about $1,500 to get the coin mold made and a decent amount to start out with. I needed to know how many other items to get to raffle off. I wanted to get them made before our director retired so we could put a decent coin on his plaque. As he handled the shotgun, he attempted to clear it, but rather than clearing, a round discharged up into the ceiling. Needless to say, we were all shocked. We had been on plenty of ranges, and had plenty of bullets fly over our heads, but none of us could have predicted what had just happened.

He said, "Well, it's cleared now," and placed the gun back in its case. He was a contractor, so he fell under local law enforcement, and he would be sentenced to community service. My fate would be different. I could stay angry at decisions made, or I could accept the fact that some higher power, someone other than myself, had other plans for me and was guiding those decisions. This was an accident, which happens all the time in our community. We deal with it internally, and it generally doesn't end careers. But I wasn't in my community, I was on my own. I was in a world run by civilians who were all lost in a paper shuffle. We were away from the agency, within a fenced compound, and nobody came in unless we let them in.

It happened on a Monday morning, right before a scheduled meeting. The intelligence analyst came from the agency. The analysts would usually give us nonpertinent information, but it made them and their bosses feel good about themselves. Plus it made us appear like we were playing well with others. The analyst was in the building when the shot rang out, not that anybody from outside our building would know what a gunshot sounded like. My leadership decided to report the incident, which was the right thing to do considering the circumstances. At least, that's what leadership were telling me, but they didn't believe that either. The post police came, conducted a short investigation, took my gun, and left. They even joked about it with me as they were questioning me, saying this happens once a week in their line of work. I knew that the worst thing that would happen was I would receive a General Officer Memorandum of Reprimand (GOMAR), which wouldn't matter much at this point. I'd had a stellar career, even with all the excessive drinking. I called the USASOC CSM to let him know what was going on. What he told me would change everything.

He wanted me to keep him updated on the situation. He was disappointed, as he was one of my memorable team sergeants from fifteen years earlier and had pretty much taught me everything I needed to know to be a successful Green Beret. He mentioned in passing something about the alternate list, which is our command select list (CSL) order of merit. I corrected him and told him I wasn't eligible anymore. He corrected me right back, saying that I was the next one on the list to be activated from the year prior. This meant that he was going to activate me and give me a command position within Seventh Special Forces Group. My mind was racing and my heart was pounding. Holy crap! I was going to be a command sergeant major! I was an acting CSM three times, but this was the real deal.

Then reality hit me like a brick. I couldn't get activated with a GOMAR on my permanent file. The army frowns upon those kinds of things, and there was a possibility they would try to kick me out early. Nobody was willing to take a chance on the possibility that I might be kicked out, however unlikely that would be. Even if it came to that, I was 99 percent sure I could beat it. This was the only blemish on my twenty-six-year career.

The anger would continue to consume me, kind of like the dark force in *Star Wars*. I couldn't believe my future, my military career, could be stopped by a conventional air-force general, not even a commanding general to boot. I wasn't as rational then as I am now in writing this, although I do still have my outbursts and anxiety attacks. I have pills that help me with that little problem now. I didn't deal directly with my then-current chain of command. I only did that when I had to. The only one I trusted was a special forces major, recently an operator and a lieutenant commander navy EOD officer.

I used up all my remaining chips and assisted in the reassignment of some other SF guys there, but that was about it. I wanted to finish my career as a battalion CSM. In fact, I wanted it so bad that it would be the last fly to land on a huge pile of garbage. It would all come crashing down, just like Pink Floyd's "The Wall." I would have to wait six months before he would make a decision and decide my fate. I made the mistake of telling him, against advice, about my eventual assignment. It didn't matter; I wasn't in control. I was being guided down a path whether I was able to accept it or not. In the meantime, I continued to work, but I was going to work less and less because I was working later and later. I stopped exercising and my health was steadily declining from all the stress and increasing alcohol consumption. I was a sergeant major in special forces, so everybody assumed I was always doing something, plus I was very good at hiding my drinking problem very well.

My wife's health was getting worse, too. She was slipping into deep depression. We had a condominium in Lorton, Virginia that had three floors. It was easy for us to hide and avoid each other. They both wanted to avoid me anyway. My poor daughter spent all of her time in her small dark room. She was in chronic pain with the complications from her back condition. I wasn't paying attention to her, and I had no idea she was also slipping into deep depression. We were always on different floors, unlike today, where we are always together in the game room playing computer games. My wife and daughter didn't know how to interact with me because I was always agitated and angry. My wife was shielding my daughter from me, and they were both scared. My clouded mind seemed to think everything was normal, as long as I could get drunk. Normalcy, though, would take getting sober, therapy, and time to work on my relationships.

The USASOC CSM had his hands full with real-world issues. He was dealing with SOF all over the world, conducting various missions. We are always there—before, during, and after conflicts. We are in places the average citizen couldn't point out on the map. We are "quiet professionals," and that's how we operate. He didn't have the time to deal with me; at least that's what I thought then, and nothing has changed my mind since then. We are both retired now and haven't spoken.

The CSM did assign a soldier to deal with my reassignment. I was out processing the unit whenever I managed to show up; otherwise, I was at home drinking. I was outside the umbrella of the special operations command (SOCOM) and was pretty much on my own. My clouded mind was convinced that everybody was out to get me. Nobody within my current unit was going to jeopardize careers or retirement to help me, even though this was where they put the misfits who wouldn't be commanders or CSMs. I was, potentially, the only one who could break that mold. I had a job interview for another position, so I could hide out until that hiring decision was made. If it went my way, I could disappear from there without anybody noticing. Unfortunately, the interview didn't go well. I guess I was acting a bit irrational, according to my interviewer. No shit! I was very close to a breakdown, and I am sure I looked terrible.

Needless to say, I didn't get that job. I would find out later that the same guy that said I was unstable made a few phone calls on my behalf, because it definitely appeared to him that I didn't have any support, and I needed it. He wasn't even in my community, but he still remembered how to take care of soldiers, a lost art. I would see him eight months later in the transition center. That was my last official day in the military, and he was starting the process for retirement. I guess I didn't look as disheveled, because we stared at each other for a few moments until he recognized me. I didn't recognize him, though, and that is still a problem I am dealing with, having received a few traumatic brain injuries throughout the years. I was also thirty-six pounds lighter, and he was happy to see me looking better. That's when he told me he had made some inquiries on my behalf.

I was a bit irrational, angry, and reckless during this period. There was a nice path running through the woods behind the compound that a few of us liked to run on. The paths there were excellent for running: good uneven ground, mixed in with wood platforms, bridges spanning gaps, steep hills, and beautiful scenery. It was normally very serene and relaxing. It was storming one day, a good one with lightning strikes. I was feeling exceptionally agitated and decided to go for a run. I had found out that the agency suspended my security clearance, standard procedure when one is under investigation, but I had already gone far enough down that path of destruction not to let that bother me. I knew all the proper procedures, which were set in place to protect the government and the individual. I had been on the other side of the situation many, many times. The post issued alerts about the storm that was pummeling the area, and it was a good one; all nonessential personal were sent home, which usually means everybody except a few. Lightning and high winds had already downed trees and power lines. I decided I was going to go on a run anyway. I didn't realize it at the time, like so many unfortunate souls don't, but I was definitely taking a risk, a sure sign of trouble and a cry for help. I had seen that so many times in my career, and it is up there on the list of things to look for to prevent suicides. I am fortunate that I didn't find what I was looking for, as that memory of running down the paths, spooked animals looking for safety, the winds, the lightning strikes, and the all-encompassing rage that drove me through the forest will forever haunt me.

The decision had finally been made. I was going to find out my fate after a long six months. I had gained too much weight and couldn't fit into my dress jacket, so I had to buy a new one, proving I was a good soldier all the way until the end; plus it would probably look bad to be busting out of the seams and popping buttons while I was in there. I was hopeful the General Officer would do the right thing, at least to get rid of me. Why would he piss off SOCOM? I knew I was reeking of alcohol, but I didn't care. I would either be departing immediately for Florida or not.

My future was in the hands of somebody who knew absolutely nothing about special operations. He was a pilot, for God's sake. I don't ever remember being so angry, and I couldn't even think straight when he handed down his decision. Now remember, a GOMAR is only a counseling statement from a general officer. Normally I wouldn't give a shit, but this was so very different. He gave me the typical, conventionalized justification about how he came to his decision; I had heard it all before. Hell, I probably used some of the same rhetoric from time to time, but I didn't hear any of it now. I was in there alone. I didn't want any of my chain of command with me, either. I trusted very few colleagues in my then-current state of mind. Besides, the issue was between the General Officer and me. I wasn't going to take a battalion; that was all I could think about.

He rambled on, and I started having dangerous thoughts. I was gripping the chair, deciding on whether I was going to jump over the desk and kill him. I know now that I wouldn't have been be able to stop once I started. He wasn't stupid though; he had his civilian boss in there. I could have easily taken them both. I know now that it would have been wrong, but still my anger is building up in me as I write this. It would have taken more than simply his boss to stop me. I thank God to this day that I didn't act on my impulse, and I still don't know what kept me from doing it either. I wasn't thinking about my family or jail time. I just didn't. Of course, going to jail after assaulting a General Officer wouldn't have helped my family, me, or my career.

I think I said some things on my behalf. I don't remember. But it doesn't matter; it wouldn't have changed his decision. The funny thing is that I have no idea if the GOMAR ever even made it into my permanent records. It would have gone in my Official Military Personnel Files (OMPF). I never saw it in there, though, and that crap doesn't go on your DD-214, which is your military career all summed up on a few pages—thanks for your service, here is what you kind of did, now get out. Basically, I retired before the Agency could even file it. I got up, saluted, and stormed out. My civilian boss was standing outside. He asked me how it went, and I disrespectfully didn't stop, talking to him over my shoulder as I very quickly walked away. I went outside and sat in my truck, steaming. I had to stop thinking about how I was going to hurt this individual physically. I could go home and get a weapon; this whole thing started with a bang, and I could end it with one. I gained enough composure to call the USASOC CSM to let him know the verdict. My next stop was the liquor store.

I got home in the afternoon and immediately began power drinking. Two hours later, I was in bad shape. Anger and rage can fuel the alcoholic's ability to consume, like a supervillian I thought I was the victim. It is never your fault, right? All the memories over the years came flooding back: my childhood, every bad decision I made drunk, all the bad decisions I made wanting to get to that point, before my military career and after.

I was no longer in control. Alcohol was my master. I was in a haze. I looked down and saw my wife's .357 Taurus revolver resting on my lap. My gun case was upstairs on the third floor. I'd had a blackout, and it had been a while since I had one of those. I walked upstairs and got the case, and I couldn't recall ever doing that. I had decided I was going to end it. I wasn't in control.

I loaded the revolver with the hollow points that I must have also brought downstairs. I tried to seat the chamber, but something was jamming it. Had it been seated and good to go when it was on my lap? I stripped it down over and over, but it wouldn't seat. I threw it down on the floor in anger. I would find out later that the firing pin was bent. How could it get bent from me just loading rounds?

I don't remember getting the Taurus, but I do remember getting my 9 mm Beretta. I picked up the pieces of the weapon, unlocked the door, and opened it. My wife was standing there and my daughter was on the stairwell. My wife saw the revolver but, thankfully, my daughter didn't. I gave the revolver to my wife and said, "it doesn't work." I saw them clear as day. The haze was gone. What the hell was I doing?

I came to my senses, but I lost control of my emotions. My wife took me outside in the backyard, and I broke down. I vaguely remember calling the USASOC CSM, but those memories are jumbled. That was my first cry for help. I handed the phone over to my wife, and he gave her instructions, which included removing all the weapons from the home.

I didn't go back to work, and nobody bothered to check up on me, even after the phone call I made. I was a master at hiding my problems. I spent the next month or so acting like nothing happened. My wife was terrified I would do something stupid again. I continued to drink heavily. My garage on the bottom floor smelled like alcohol and urine. I wouldn't even bother to go upstairs to use the bathroom; instead, I would piss in plastic bottles. I had done that in Afghanistan, but then I would dispose of the bottles the next day.

My poor wife was getting worse by the day and my daughter started cutting herself. We didn't realize that until months later. My daughter was on her own. She had to get herself up in the morning and get ready for school; we wouldn't even bother to get up. She even had to feed herself most of the time. My wife was sleeping all day because she was exhausted from staying up all night watching me to make sure I didn't die in my sleep. What kind of provider was I?

I was diagnosed with sleep apnea right before I got out. That, mixed with alcohol, is bad news. I was always very good at pushing all the bad stuff deep within my subconscious so that I never had to deal with it. Alcoholism is a disease, but there are always underlying reasons why you continue to kill yourself.

I was a terrible father and husband, and I spend every day trying to make amends and repair the damage I caused with my immediate family. I still haven't been able to focus any further than that. I keep being told by therapists, doctors, and Alcoholics Anonymous buddies that I have a unique gift to offer individuals in my community. I am just not ready yet. I still don't know why my wife didn't leave me. I hinted at it enough, and she definitely would have been better off without me. I am blessed to still have her, my daughter, and my son in my life. I certainly don't deserve and didn't earn it, but I am still working on that part.

My future was an empty void. I wasn't planning for anything; all I lived for was to get drunk, and I did that all the time. I was spending thousands of dollars each month on it. One night, my body finally revolted and decided to give me a wakeup call by stopping my breathing. That was scary, but was it scary enough to stop drinking? Hell no! My wife had to help me get dressed and take me to the emergency room, an all-too- common occurrence.

I think my daughter was waiting for me to leave this earth. Rank might have its privileges (RHIP), but not if you really need help. I had spent many years helping service members, civilians, and their families, but I didn't know how to ask for help myself. I know I smelled like a brewery in the emergency room, but nobody said anything. The doctor put me on a breather to help open up my lungs, and then eventually sent me home with a clean bill of health. Are you kidding me? That was my second cry for help, and it wouldn't be the last either. As a leader, I was always able to spot the signs in others. Why wasn't anybody seeing them in me? Could I be that good at hiding them at this late stage?

The third cry for help happened with my primary-care manager (PCM). I went to see him, but I can't remember why. I think it was for a spot on my lungs or something. I don't know what came over me, but I simply just started unloading all my problems on him. He would become the first person I ever told about how much, and how long, I had been drinking. My wife's jaw dropped, and the young captain's eyes looked like he was having information overload. My fifteen-minute appointment turned into an hour and a half. I still didn't get any help. I even told him I tried to kill myself a month prior, as well as about the amounts of alcohol I was consuming. He asked if I still wanted to hurt myself or others. I wasn't going to admit any of that yet. He only asked me to try to get some help and, that if I did decide to get help, to call him anytime. I should have been admitted then and there. Crazy, huh? That wouldn't even happen for two more weeks.

I look back on pictures from this time and, boy, do I look terrible. I was slowly killing myself, and I couldn't get any help. I stayed home for another two weeks. I was in denial. I had a talk with my wife and decided I was going to have to do it myself.

So I went into work and talked to one of the officers I trusted. It was a Thursday, and it would be the last day I would drink. I went into work and confessed. It was a four-day weekend, so I told him I was going to wait until Monday and admit myself to the hospital for detoxification. I don't think this was registering with him at first. After all, I was a sergeant major. We don't have problems—we help solve everybody else's. This was my fourth cry for help in forty-five days, but this one would be answered.

He consulted with his superiors; I wonder how that conversation went. He called me back that evening and, of course, I was drunk. He asked me, "If you are going to admit yourself, why wait until Monday?" He had a point, and he was right; I wouldn't have done it. He told me to come into work the next day, and we would talk about it. but I was never going to return there and talk with those individuals.

I got so mad, I decided to admit myself that night. I would show them! I know now that if I hadn't done it, I probably would have been command-referred anyway. The result of that process would be very different. I told my wife to drive me to the hospital. My doctor told me to come see him when I was ready. That was exactly what I was going to do.

However, I changed my mind immediately. I had plenty of alcohol in the house and felt it shouldn't go to waste, right? It was a long night of drinking, and I finally passed out around two o'clock in the morning. I got up three hours later because I could never sleep very well anyway. I woke my wife and told her I was ready to do it.

CHAPTER 7

Institutionalized

My wife had to drive me because I was still drunk. She hated driving for me, though, because I criticized every move and decision she made. I have considerably more patience now, but the damage was done, and she will probably never be comfortable driving for me.

I was angry and anxious. I wasn't in control, and it made me uncomfortable. I had no idea how this was going to turn out. I'd had my share of soldiers in this situation, but found it was definitely a little more stressful when the roles were reversed.

She parked in the hospital garage, and I immediately started yelling at her. She didn't do or say anything to deserve it; I was grasping for excuses not to go through with it. There were people there staring at us, and once again my better half was embarrassed. But she stayed strong, took the verbal punishment, and waited patiently to hand me off to somebody who could better deal with me. I was panicking a little bit, feeling like a cornered rat. Was I really going to stop drinking?

We walked up to the secretary behind the desk and asked for my doctor. Of course, being a typical government worker and not wanting to get all the information, she said we couldn't see him without an appointment. She actually refused to get him! Who in their right mind would want socialized medicine! I was a bit frustrated but, hell, if he wasn't going to see me, I could go home, right? Instead, my wife led me to the emergency room.

There was definitely no turning back now. I walked in, gave them my ID card, and answered the big question of the day. Why I was there? Well, at least it was better than the alternative. This was voluntary, after all. I told them that I needed to detox, that I couldn't control my drinking, and that I needed some help. The nurse looked at me funny, as I guess they don't see too many sergeant majors walking in and confessing that. However, when it does happen, it is serious.

It didn't take long to get a bed in there; that was a relief, because it generally takes a few hours before they will see you. But I am guessing I ranked high enough on the triage flowchart to get in right away. I started talking to the nurse, and she was filling out some paperwork, but then my wife mentioned that my primary-care manager was expecting me and that he already had all my information. He showed up an hour or so later and began the inpatient process.

There were quite a few side conversations between my wife and the hospital staff, and I was still drunk and not very talkative. I didn't know it then, but I would run into the on-duty physician a few months later in the emergency room. I wouldn't remember her, but she remembered me.

My appearance was terrible, and I was overweight; my memory was shot, and my vocabulary wasn't as extensive as it once was. The medical treatment I received at this particular hospital was excellent; it certainly wasn't an assembly line of broken bones like down at Fort Bragg. And they put up with my bad behavior. I am not sure if it was my rank or because they just had excellent bedside manners. But either way, I was appreciative, especially after I started getting my senses back. I still didn't know what to expect at this point, but at least I was there with no chance of turning back. I was there for the long haul, and it was brutal at times. After all, I had been drinking since my teen years. The staff got me checked in and moved me out of the emergency room into a hospital room sometime in the late afternoon. I would be monitored twenty-four hours a day during my stay in that wing.

There is a distinct difference between coming off—let's say—pills or heroine versus alcohol. You can quit the latter cold turkey. Symptoms may include body and muscle aches, vomiting, and mood disorders like anxiety or depression, but as long as you don't harm yourself you should be OK. In my case, I came in extremely intoxicated, and doctors needed to monitor me in order preserve respiration and cardiovascular function until the alcohol levels fell into a safe range. In other words, during a severe case of intoxication, one can stop breathing or the heart can stop beating. Drinking or taking drugs is usually harmless at first. But once your body builds a tolerance to it and becomes dependent on it, it's necessary to address both medical and mental problems that compel continued usage. In my case, once my body was free from alcohol, the work of looking inside began.

They kept me on a steady dosage of valium, and after a few days I was having problems. I didn't enjoy taking the medication because it made me constipated. Probably the biggest reason I didn't become addicted to painkillers is because that was when my headaches started; I was impacted before and it wasn't a pleasant experience. I was pleasantly high, but I would soon pay the price. They also had a few different yellow-looking cocktails pumping into my veins. This was the standard protocol, to blast my body with vitamins and electrolytes and keep me somewhat hydrated.

They assigned a female sergeant medical technician to watch me around the clock to make sure I didn't die. I am sure there were others, but she is the only one I remember. I must have been pretty impressed with her, because I kept trying to convince her to attend Ranger School. I also gave her my fiftieth anniversary Seventh Special Forces Group coin—I was wondering where that went! My wife stayed with me on and off whenever she felt comfortable leaving our daughter alone. I had some visitors from the hospital staff, none of whom I remember. They spoke to my wife; one was a chaplain whom I would meet again in a few months, and the other was a therapist from the addiction clinic to see if I was a candidate.

Somehow, I bypassed a considerable waiting list and got in right after I was deemed safe and alcohol was officially out of my system. I would be the first special forces sergeant major to be admitted. The staff later told me that the original intent of the program was to help long-term users, like myself, to reintegrate, either back into the military or to transition to the next chapter in life. I definitely fit that description.

I am glad I was admitted. Addicts help themselves by helping others, and I needed all the help I could get. It was imperative that I get better, or I would never be able to help my family.

I actually helped a lot of service members just by being there and wanting to get better, still setting the example, definitely a lost art even in the best circumstances. It felt good to be able to affect others positively again from my actions. Plus, they all looked up to me because of my rank and were impressed with what I did for a living. After all, nobody there was exactly a killer. They were great people and everybody plays their part, whatever role one plays in the armed forces.

The day before I was to be transferred, I started getting constipated from the valium and the cramps began. Oh no, here we go again. How do people deal with this as addicts? At least alcohol kept me regular! My wife brought me a quart of prune juice, and I slammed the whole thing. That was a big mistake. I would go through phases of severe cramps, and I couldn't lay on the bed or sit down. I do remember wanting to lie on the cool linoleum floor in the latrine. The hospital staff frowned on that. Why? It is in a hospital and it's clean, right? I refused to get up, so the staff had to get me up off the floor and walk me to the bed. I leaned on it until the bout with cramps passed. I only remember bits and pieces of what transpired during the detox period, but the cramps I will never forget. I was also still in my sweats because I refused to put on a hospital gown. I was a bad patient, and I must have stunk pretty good by that point.

It was now time to transition from the detox ward to the addiction clinic. I was simply going through the motions at this point, absent-mindedly filling out the paperwork and answering questions. What I do remember is, yet again, refusing to get out of my clothes and into a hospital gown. It is standard procedure to wear one for the first twenty-four hours so the staff can pick you out of a crowd right away in case there are problems. I went into the latrine outside the office and threw the gown out the door. The staff went with it because they didn't want to fight with me. I can't remember if my wife was with me when I checked in, but I suppose she was because she got a packing list of stuff I was authorized to keep with me. I had a bag, but I couldn't keep half the stuff that was in it, and that pissed me off. My humbling was coming.

The following real-life scenario was just like being in jail. I was in jail for a bit in Ajo, Arizona, and in Mexico, but I don't remember much of that. The set up of the ward had three sets of locked doors: the first came into the lobby, the second opened up into our common area, and the last led into our sleeping areas. There were medical technicians posted everywhere, but if anything were to really get out of control, they could call for some help from the ward across the way or the hospital's armed security guards. The only thing I remember from my first night in there was being curled up in a ball in a corner of the common area. I was under a window, wishing I was dead because of the pain in my gut. They were trying to offer me natural remedies—prune juice and herbal teas—but soon realized how futile that was. There was no way I was drinking anymore prune juice! Eventually, they called up a prescription and gave me the good stuff. It was some strange, white-colored liquid in a bottle. I drank that and went to my room to wait. I defecated a few times that night, but I went eight times the next day before noon. The other patients and staff were amused.

I didn't go to the gym that first morning, but I did notice the uniform for patients was your service-specific physical fitness attire. The duty uniform was your service-specific uniform, and we were able to wear civilian attire after 5:00 p.m. It was a joint facility, and it was interesting to me to see all the armed forces represented in one area. Even though we each had our own demons, the one thing we all had in common was some form of addiction. I knew there was widespread alcoholism in the military, but I was surprised to find out how much drug use there was and still is. I saw everything from painkillers and heroin addiction to alcoholism. We were all in different stages of denial, but we would become lifelong friends trying to help each other.

My routine day consisted of getting up at a quarter past four in the morning. I would review the bible and the Alcoholics Anonymous teachings for the day. I would read the Serenity Prayer: "God grant me the serenity to accept the things I cannot change; courage to change the things I can; and the wisdom to know the difference." I would then read a prayer from St. Francis, which is posted in *Twelve Steps and Twelve Traditions*. It reads: "Lord, make me a channel of thy peace - that where there is hatred, I may bring love - that where there is wrong, I may bring the spirit of forgiveness - that where there is discord, I may bring harmony - that where there is error, I may bring the truth - that where there is doubt, I may bring faith - that where there is despair, I may bring hope - that where there are shadows, I may bring light - that where there is sadness, I may bring joy. Lord, grant that I may seek rather to comfort than to be comforted - to understand, than to be understood - to love, than to be loved. For it is by self-forgetting that one finds. It is by forgiving that one is forgiven. It is by dying that one awakens to eternal life, Amen."

All of these readings gave me the power to focus all my strength on learning what I needed to do to stay sober so I could help my family. We were given a urinalysis every Monday, which would become my routine up until the day I became a civilian. We would meander into the common room, where a medical technician took our temperature and blood pressure. I was always first, until a certain marine gunnery sergeant showed up. The others took medications to help them sleep. I would prefer to wear myself out, so I that was ready to pass out each night. We would then be escorted down to the van and shuttled to one of the post gyms. We were always supervised and had our special hospital wristbands, which identified who we were. Some of the patients worked out and some would find a secluded spot and get some more sleep, a different generation I guess. Exercise is very important to recovery. One of the doctors told me that, if one continues to exercise regularly, the body's chemistry will stabilize in five years, otherwise it would take eight years.

I needed the shorter time frame, I had a lot of catching up to do, and I needed to get better so I could be of some use to my family. I was too old to continue drinking, and I could use all the help I could get. We would return from the gym, shower, get into our uniforms, and then meet in the common room to eat breakfast. My uniform was tight; it would become too big a month later. The rest of the day consisted of learning how to cope with our addictions. I learned considerably more than I was expecting. I learned how to meditate, to calm my mind and to help ease the passing of cravings. We had some sort of meditation every day. It was very quiet in the wing. I would not be able to sleep with the television on in my room anymore. Today, the wife and I use our phones and iPads, but when it is time to sleep everything is shut off. I learned how to get some of my aggression out on paper. I didn't like to draw or paint, but I did enjoy writing poems, which was very helpful. Chapter 8 of this book is dedicated to my writings while in therapy. I enjoyed my time in art therapy as well; don't call it art class or the therapist will correct you. I didn't initially, but it grew on me.

We had a physical therapist who took us to the pool once a week. It was a great time to take out some needed frustrations by trying to drown each other in the deep end. I learned Hai Chi, too, which is Tai Chi only in the water. My coordination was improving, but I had a hard time in yoga. Still, I felt at peace while I was performing the movements in the pool.

I learned a Japanese form of meditation called Reiki. There is no scientific explanation as to why it works, and it certainly doesn't work for everybody. I guess it is like a voodoo curse. If you believe you are cursed, then you subconsciously have whatever symptoms are related to it. I found quite a few alternative methods for coping, ones that have been tested and are known to work. Those would be Alcoholics Anonymous (AA), the Twelve Steps, and sponsorship. Nobody is going to understand what you are going through like another alcoholic that has been there and done that. We attended mandatory meetings for AA and Narcotics Anonymous, both of which were quite helpful. Both employ the same teachings that addicts have been using to get and stay sober since the 1930s. We would eat lunch in the cafeteria, a chance to get out of confinement and mingle with the rest of the hospital population. The recreational therapist would take us around the outside of the hospital, to walk off our chow so we wouldn't be falling asleep the rest of the afternoon. The recreational therapy consisted of developing a plan to occupy free time and filling the gaps with activities to avoid thinking about addiction. We played games that helped with team building and muscle and hand-eye coordination. The therapist would monitor us to see where we were and helped us adjust our plans accordingly.

The counselor who stood out the most gave us our daily dose of needed reality. He was teamed up with various chaplains who monitored both him and us. This is where the first three steps of the AA twelve-step program was beaten into our heads. If a patient was in denial, then it was his or her time to shine. No feelings were spared, and every single one of us hated him at one time or another during those twenty-eight days, but it was the best counseling I received. Being nice and sweet has its place in rehab, but when you want to get a point across to an addict in the midst of a craving, make it a concrete experience. He was the one who focused me on retirement and taking care of my "unit," or family, and that nothing was more important. I was done with the military, and it was time to get better and move on. I had been conditioned to be in the military for twenty-seven years and, at this point, I needed a little help breaking me out of my obsession. I heard later that they removed this portion of the program; what a shame. The success rate will decline without it.

Having an entire "touchy-feely" program isn't a good idea, especially for members of the armed forces. Hard-ass, concrete experiences is what we need. I was running and doing sit-ups every night in the very small hallway near our rooms. Those activities, along with the gym and the pool thrown in once a week, helped me sleep at night. It was easy to focus on physical fitness, since I was locked up and couldn't venture out anyway. I was even able to convince the staff to take us out on runs in the evening before dinner. I was really making a difference, getting better at the same time, and getting in decent shape by the time I started outpatient therapy.

I came to the realization that I couldn't keep up with the same lifestyle, and that I had to have a drastic lifestyle change. Some of the patients and nurses thought I had "wet brain" when I first showed up. It is a common term for Wernicke-Korsakoff syndrome, basically that my brain was being starved of thiamine. It caused me to have some loss of control of my right eye, confusion, memory loss, and hallucinations. Remember the ghosts I thought were inhabiting my previous home? I was seeing and hearing things in my hospital room at night too, and I couldn't sleep with my back to the room. I am glad that doesn't happen anymore.

I had good days and bad days in rehab. During one of my paranoid delusions, I was actually convinced that a patient was putting drugs in my water bottles. I even addressed this with the on-duty psych and asked him to give me a urinalysis. Of course, it was all in my mind, but I thought it was reality. Relapse is a part of recovery. There are many phases, but that's one I would have been more than happy to bypass.

The calculated success rate from this particular program was 10 percent. That seems about right, now that I think about who has relapsed and recovered and who has relapsed and not recovered. So far, only two of my original group of twenty or so are still sober without a relapse, knock on wood.

I would go to church every Sunday. There was a Catholic mass at half past nine in the morning. My wife and daughter would come to the hospital and attend. I even had a reconciliation with the priest. It had been a long time since I turned my back on God, and it was time to bring him back into my life.

Periodically, an officer would come from my chain of command to get an update on my progress, one of the two officers I trusted. I hadn't gotten to the point of realizing that most of my circumstances stemmed from my actions. I was still upset about the incident. Everybody knew I was going to retire. I was getting the time I needed to get better, get my life together, and transition into civilian life. I still don't know if it was directed from higher. I do know that nobody from outside my section within the agency ever checked up on me, and only a few from within even knew I was there. It seemed as if the art of taking care of soldiers was lost on my behalf.

I received counseling, therapy, or both in some way each day. I had a brand new, young navy doctor who was working with me, and sometimes my humor was lost on him.! They had me take myriad psychological exams and evaluations. The therapist administering them to me was crying right alongside me when I was telling my story. If there is one thing I want the reader to get out of this chapter, it's that the military health system has come a long way in helping its Armed Forces personnel cope and recover from addiction. Don't let it get to the point I did and waste all those golden years suffering. Embrace the Alcoholics Anonymous Twelve Step Program but, even more importantly, you have to want to stop. You know if you have a problem; I did too. You have to come to the realization that you can live a happy, comfortable life without your chosen substance. There is help out there. Don't worry about how it will affect your career. Your health and well-being are more important. I wasted many years, and I have a long way to go. This was my first step in living a new life, a better life where I can function and take care of my family. I am and always will be an alcoholic, but the difference is that I can cope now. This program helped me focus on staying sober, but it didn't address any of the underlying reasons as to why I was drinking. My doctor decided I should continue with my therapy in trauma and substance abuse with the Warrior Transition Unit. I would report the day after I was discharged. My addiction was doing pushups in the parking lot. It was strong and patiently waiting for me to leave the hospital. I would be tested as soon as I drove home.

CHAPTER 8
Writings

The following are writings and poems I created while I was in rehab and therapy. Rehabilitation and art therapy opened my mind and allowed me to cleanse my soul and ease some of the pain by getting it out and onto paper. They do not appear in any particular sequence or chronological order, mainly because that time was a blur. Post-traumatic stress affects the left and right sides of the brain, making it difficult to differentiate between what is happening right this moment and past events. This is a problem that I, among many others associated with our military service, am afflicted with and have to deal with every day. It will never go away, but it can be tolerated once the events can be sequenced. I am including notes to help you, the reader, understand what was going on in my head. Poems are a form of art, and thus are interpreted differently for each reader, depending on life experiences and even something as simple as a mood change. I wrote these in a stressful and uncertain period in my life. To me, they are therapeutic, and I relive the events each time I read them. It gets easier each time.

Those We Left Behind

This is for all those that have given the ultimate sacrifice
You served and left behind your loved one's paying the ultimate price
Be at peace, we will never forget, your families will forever be taken care of
One day the world will be at peace, the crow will die and forever free will be the dove

Note: Our community would never leave anybody behind unless it was unpreventable. We do deploy all over the world and leave our families back home. It is imperative that they cared for, so that we can focus on the mission, even in our passing. Some of my comrades have departed physically, but they will be reunited with their families and loved ones one day. We maintain relationships, the best we can, with these families. It is easier for some of us. Our community will always be there for them in their times of need. I doubt that we will ever see the last line of the poem on this earth. Man will always be at war and continue to profit off the misfortunes of others. There will be no Valhalla for our fallen comrades, but there will always be heaven.

<u>The Crow</u>
I have seen this crow
standing atop the gravestone
I know it's the same crow
because of the battle scars
marking its claws and beak
I have seen this crow
when I bury a comrade
It stares at the
crowd, the casket then me
I hate seeing the crow
every time I lay a comrade to rest
I know it's the same crow
because of the battle scars
marking its claws and beak
I have tried to kill the
crow but it always eludes me
I have lost my faith along
the way, the crow is always
there when I visit my comrades
maybe if I regain my faith
the crow will go away but for the time being
I have lost my way

Note: This poem describes my pain and anguish each time I performed a funeral for one of my own. The crow is death, the enemy, the darkness where I was hiding my guilt. I was already broken inside when I moved on to where I wasn't exposed to constant death and grief. I could no longer deal with it, so I stopped interacting with my peers except at work, and I could no longer go to anymore funerals, combat related or not.

<u>Sleep</u>

Although I have cleared my mind and soul I still cannot sleep
I must learn to be calm and rational, but I am a wolf in a world of sheep
I carry many battle scars and thoughts of places far away
I am restless and weary, it is time to forgive and keep those demons at bay
I feel the urge to run with the pack, but I am an outcast and alone
I am older, wiser and more cunning and my foundation is still stone
It is time for me to rest, take care of myself
Maybe, just maybe I can learn to be calm and rational,
hide among the masses, a wolf dressed as a sheep
I have cleared my mind and soul, maybe now I can sleep

Note: This describes my struggle with my coming to terms with retirement and the next chapter in my life. My days of wondering where and when I was getting drunk were over. Putting words into action was a difficult task, as all I knew was the army and special forces. The easy out would be to continue working for the government, similar to the majority of my peers and seniors in the past. I had to do something as a veteran, but I also wanted to be happy doing it; and that wasn't anything related to what I had done for the past twenty-eight years.

Coping

I can't feel, remember or experience without wanting a drink
I know what I must do but the things I have done have brought me to this brink
Is it easier to kill than to write a poem? I am still not sure.
One I was taught and done quite well the other I discovered when my mind was a
blur
I was taken to the hospital, determined but not alone because I couldn't walk
I yearn for freedom from the drink, to be with my family, with God
but I am behind a lock
I'm learning to cope one day at a time
it is easy here, controlled, monitored but what will I do when I step on the first mine
I want to and I need to be sober for eternity
I have everything to live for and everything to lose, I must maintain sobriety
so here I sit making this list of mechanisms to help me cope
unconventional methods like reiki, Ah'chi, and similar activities I will have that will
give me my hope
I will have AA, church, and its community as many a building stone
but the higher power as I understand it, has been there and always will be, thanks
be to God I am not alone

Note: This one is pretty clear and to the point. Even now that I am sober, I still regrettably cannot answer the question "Is it easier to kill than to write a poem?" I do thank God every day that he has allowed me to walk a healthier and happier path.

<u>Forgiveness</u>
I grew up in turmoil and disarray
I had no direction I had lost my way
I met my soul mate who had direction
I take the leap of faith thinking I made a revelation
but I was always lost, I thought I believed but could not forgive
from the things that had happened to me, my life I could not quite love
I lost myself in alcohol, I thought it would make things better
but all it was doing was slowly killing my soul, I was moving through mud, my mind
was wetter
I know now I must forgive, I used to believe but now I know
I can be happy again with an external and internal glow

Note: Here is my struggle with religion. My mother is Catholic. She practices now, but she didn't raise me as one even though I was baptized in the Church. After I met my second wife, I became immersed in the church. I liked it because it had structure just like the military. A buddy of mine, also a Green Beret, brought me into the Church under an adult program to help me through the process I would have gone through as a child. Unfortunately, I was only going through the motions, and my heart was never truly in it. I was married by church a year or so after our magistrate wedding. I turned my back on God around 2008, and I have been struggling to get him back in my life ever since my reconciliation in rehab. I know what I must do, that it is the right thing to do, but I can't seem to focus my life in that direction.

The Answer
Do I need to drink?
Not if I want to survive.
I have my answer!

Coping
Is it time to learn
What is the mechanism?
It is time to cope

Daughter
I love my daughter
She means everything to me
My Elizabeth

Note: This was my first attempt at writing haiku poems, which consist of three non-rhyming lines, with each subsequent line containing a different number of syllables. The first and last contain five, the second contains seven.

Good-Bye

The beast that was in control has been laid to rest
It hides in the shadows waiting to pounce
It has the ability to destroy the strongest of bonds
to confuse the scholar to prevent the mother from returning to her nest
It clouds the mind with its breath and with its claws destroys reason
the beast hides in plain sight, always at arm's length
it instills fear and confuses every and all emotions
is it cold? hot? warm? freezing? lost in the past the blending of every season
I will never be able to say goodbye, it will always be there
can I live like this?
I will continue on! for me, for them
I can say goodbye while I keep it at bay, for short periods of time, I will not peer
over my shoulder or stare

Note: This is my wife's favorite poem. Here, I am saying goodbye to my addiction. I will always be an alcoholic but, as long as I stay vigilant and focused, I can maintain a new and improved life without it.

First Three Steps

Step 1
yes, "I" am honest!
It's "I" now, but always we!
yes, I do need help.

Step 2
Deflate your ego
stay sober, I want to live!
open mindedness

Transition
I will stay sober
we must rally together
it's time to move on

Step 3
Must have willingness
Become dependent on God
Always trust the path

Note: Haiku poems again, showing my understanding of the first three steps of the twelve-step process. These were beaten into my brain during my twenty-eight-day re-hab stay. Remember, Bill and Bob have been helping people with this since the 1930s, and it works. You just have to want to stop drinking.

<u>Reborn</u>

I didn't know I could get close to another human being
to let down my guard, show that I care, allow my soul to be seen
my life was always so cloudy, full of blood and forever tormented
now it is clear, I can see their shroud, their halo, both are uplifted
I always knew love was there from my life partner and children
I strive to return what I have learned, for this I am driven
my past is full of hate, remorse, and resentment
but I know now, a choice must be made, the righteous path or a wrongful
commitment
I can't do this alone, I tried and failed so many times in the past
I opened myself up to those willing to help, from beginning to last

Note: I had hidden my problems and addiction for so long that it was an enormous re-lief to finally let down my guard and just talk to somebody about it. More importantly, to open up, be humble, and accept the help that offered.

<u>Tormented</u>

How could something that happened to me so many years ago be associated with someone who wasn't even born

events that intertwine from three unrelated parts, a death, abuse, and not knowing

a death that was unforeseen but necessary then, I see his face, I see my face, so much guilt

he was abused, she knew, but turned a cheek, lifestyle changes and a path would be broken from stone

I didn't know then like I do now, I knew it wasn't my fault, but irrational thoughts prevail

why do I see his face, totally unrelated but a truth, why do I continue down a dark path when he has forgiven

somehow I must forgive myself before accepting forgiveness, I ask for help because I am lost and see no discernible path to the light

the left and the right can't recollect, the sequence of events doesn't make any sense, the more I write maybe the more real it will become

Note: Here I talk about an incident that happened in South America and how it eventually affects my relationship with my son. I describe the abuse he suffered under his mother's care and how I can't tie any of it together; even though prior events have affected my decisions, it is all a jumbled mess.

<u>I Am</u>
I am what I have done
but mostly what was done to me
the beast manifested itself at an early age
was it predestined? or predisposition?
the memories come and go
now that I am out of the haze
when will the pain and suffering become healing?
it is so difficult being less resilient and aged
I want to see the light
not only for self-preservation, but for them
the ones that were always there
I couldn't see, wouldn't see, I had no control
but, here they are still standing beside me
I am grateful while receiving strength to do what I have to do
to make things right
I must process what was done to me
I am what I have done

Note: I am describing my journey through the different stages of alcoholism. I have been told, based on the events that happened to me as a child, that I was predisposed to be an addict. I had to focus on getting healthy and staying alive so I could take care of my family.

The Boy

The boy felt a presence, very late one night
not a glimmer of hope but of violence and despair
these things were done to him, bringing down the darkness
not a time of peace, no protection from the womb
the boy faded and pushed everything over the horizon
away from the dawn

The boy became a man, but did he?
thus the crow entered his life, judging all his decisions
turning his back on God, empowering the blackness
giving in to evil, feeding the addiction
a new chapter in his life, confusion, self-centeredness, a deep empty space

Nothing around his body is familiar, but inside quite insane
can this be the end for this man, but is it?
can the crow be forgotten, what was the presence?
the man saw as a boy
these things he will never forget, but must learn how to live
wave away the violence and despair and embrace spark, the glimmer of hope

Note: This is a nonrhyming poem. I still have a vivid memory, right before my appendix became inflamed, of a demon-like creature walking into my room and standing at my dresser. I was on the bottom bunk, sharing the space with someone, my back up against the wall. I got up on an elbow, and the creature looked at me and smiled. I was frozen in fear. I managed to dropped down and pull the covers over my head. The next thing I remember was being taken to the hospital. I don't know why I remember this. The second paragraph addresses my later years in the military, and the last one is me sobered up and trying to deal with all the pain, the underlying reasons why I drank, and just trying to live day to day.

<u>Thanks For Your Support</u>
Innocence is easily lost, but such a gift
to view the world clear, not from a programmed shift

to be free from anxiety, stress, and addiction
<u>be</u> content, <u>know</u> happiness, <u>do</u> live life without restriction

Note: This is in response to an elementary-school-aged child who wrote a very special card to service members and veterans going through hard times. The underlined words are the army's leadership model.

<u>Transition</u>

The wolf looks out into the void, the way is not clear

The bridge is thin and brittle but the new transition from wolf to sheep is here

The need to run with the pack is strong and natural, but it's not possible

The need is there to make this transition, to fit in, but is it probable

The wolf steps out onto the bridge, there is fear, stress and anxiety*

A light appears on the far end, the wolf gets distracted and howls defiantly

To make it to the end he must focus, the wolf leaps into a fierce run

He is struck on all sides, the wounds are superficial, the light becomes as bright as the sun

The wolf makes it to the end, everything appears and feels surreal

There is a clear path and one that goes into the wilds, he must trust in the path that is ideal

The path soon clears and smells of heaven, and he sees his mate with their youngling

She accepts him, he lays down beside her, the relief he feels is daunting

Note: This was the last poem I wrote. I was only able to write up to the asterisk. I completed it based on how my journey has gone since my move to North Carolina. The bridge is the journey from my military life to the next chapter, from being an alcoholic to being sober, from dealing with my past to a point where it is bearable. The wolf and youngling are my wife and daughter. I thank God every day that they are still in my life.

CHAPTER 9
Freedom

t felt surreal as I stepped outside the hospital with my wife. My unit gave my wife permission to sign me out of the addiction clinic; I didn't want any of them there anyway. She had to drive me home because I wasn't permitted to drive for twenty-four hours. I was to report to the outpatient portion the very next day. She drove me to the compound because I needed to check on the status of my retirement paperwork. I had asked my chain of command to keep an eye on it and, since I hadn't seen any e-mails, I was skeptical that anything had been done.

Of course, it never made it past the agency. My coping mechanisms were being tested, but I took a few deep breaths and decided to fend for myself from this point on. We drove to retirement services on post next. Being a sergeant major paid off, as I sat down with the retirement section and submitted all my completed paperwork in one sitting. I got a notice ten days later. The agency couldn't even get that right but, no matter, it was official now. I was getting out in eight months. I was apprehensive but at least I was thinking clearly. It was time to get serious and plan for our future. Everything from this point seemed different. I was relieved and had a positive outlook on life, but damn did I need a drink! My breakdown happening while I was on active duty had allowed me to get the help I needed. She dropped me off at home and immediately left to take my daughter to her physical therapy appointment.

I was standing at the kitchen window, looking out at the neighborhood, and it seemed so different. I looked down and saw my daughter running back up the hill toward the townhouse. I went to go meet her, and she told me they had just had a car accident. Well, it was time to put my new learned skills to the test. I love my wife more than life itself, but she has never owned a vehicle she didn't wreck at least once! I told my daughter to return to the house and calmly walked down to the scene of the accident.

I met her and the poor woman told me she had an accident. She had a look of panic on her face and was waiting for me to lose my mind, as normally that would be the case. I calmed my mind, and those who know me would be surprised. I was always known for my outbursts of anger and losing control, but instead I asked if she and the other woman were OK. They were, and then I told her that it was OK, and that we would get through this together. Her jaw dropped and relief spread across her face. It had been a long time since I "really" looked at her face. I felt terrible when I saw the look of fear and panic. It was all because of me. They were both afraid of me, and I had a long way to go to build their trust back up.

It was handled. I was calm, but my old friend was trying to tempt me and I wanted a drink. I called my sponsor; he didn't answer so I went down my list of support. I sent a text to my counselor from rehab, and we spoke until the craving subsided. The cravings only last about ten to twenty minutes, so if you can make it through that hell then you can keep the enemy at bay until the next time. That's what recovery is all about— one day at a time, even one minute at a time. I would fail if I were to forget this, stop following the path, and get too confident.

My sponsor did call me later that evening. We talked extensively, amid the mantra that you help yourself by helping others. He still wants me to help my brethren in the special operations community, and I will as soon as I get a grip on the underlying factors leading to my addiction. I am not a counselor, and I will never have a degree in that field, but I was a sergeant major in special forces and I know how to take care of service members. I will talk to anybody who will listen. He hounded me and kept me on the sober path, and I am blessed to have him and many others in my life. The phone calls and texts flowed between us on a constant and annoying basis, but that is what it is all about. Everything from this point on would be a brand new sober experience.

The addiction clinic put me on a bland but healthy diet, yogurt and such. When I returned home, my taste buds and my body couldn't handle any spices, let alone the amounts of hot sauce I used to pour all over all my food. I gagged when I ate a potato chip, as they are soaked in salt. I had to deal with my addictive behavior in other areas, and I replaced alcohol with caffeine and sugar. It started with Mountain Dew Kickstarts, and the fridge in the garage, which used to be full of beer, was now full of such sixteen-ounce cans. I would drink at least five or six per day. I figured I was OK, because at least they have some real juice in them.! Meanwhile, my appetite for food consisted of anything that wasn't healthy and was packed with sugar. It started out with Oreo cookies—a few cookies now and then, and then on to a whole package in one sitting. I went from one addiction to another. That behavior didn't affect me right away, and after all it was better than drinking. But it would a year later. I did finally kick the soda habit, it was easier than with the booze. I couldn't stop eating cookies though, it was like crack. I left the military with my teeth in pretty good shape, but after a year of that I needed some dental work.

I was nervous about checking into the Warrior Transition Unit (WTU). I was going to get the best of both worlds, though. I would get the benefits of being in the unit, but I didn't have to report there. I also chose to retire instead of being medically retired. It was nice using their facilities, especially the pharmacy. The wait time in the main hospital was two to three hours, versus ten to twenty minutes in the Warrior Pavilion. My family was able to use the services also.

My first few hours in the clinic consisted of filling out questionnaires, getting physicals, and checking in with the head nurse, the head psychiatrist, and the nurse practitioner. The latter was a captain in the air force and would be medicating me, adjusting my intake daily. I told him that I didn't feel comfortable taking medications, that in fact I had been worrying about that ever since they told me I was coming here. He said, "What's the difference? You have been self-medicating practically your entire life." I didn't know what to say except, "Touché Doc!" They started me on an injection called Vivitrol, which is a thick, milky substance that is injected into the butt muscle.

It slowly releases throughout the month to help curb cravings. It is usually prescribed in cases like mine, for an outpatient getting regular therapy. It didn't hurt going in, but it gave me one hell of a charley horse the next day, which lasted three or four additional days, and you had to alternate treatment from side to side. One should always avoiding getting it in the same cheek! I would get it for the next nine months, and it was very effective.

The staff would tell me that I should except all the help they offered, including therapy and drugs. They prescribed various medications to help me remain focused and feel somewhat normal, which I needed for depression, anxiety, headaches, and even to forget dreams. My dreams were always nightmares. I could handle the drunk dreams, but the others not so much. My body and mind were going through changes as they were healing. It was going to take some time to get used to the drugs too. I lost my appetite and that is an understatement; my body wasn't getting hungry anymore. I was the only one in my group who was losing rather than gaining weight. I had started this particular adventure weighing 226 pounds; a few months later I would weigh 185 pounds, which was about eleven pounds less than my healthy weight. The meds I took to help remedy this effect didn't take hold until a year later.

Still, this facility was a haven for me, it was place of duty, and I didn't have to worry about anything other than taking care of myself. My wife and daughter were already seeing positive changes in me, and that's all I could do at this point. I was blindly following the path before me, and everything was falling into place. I wasn't nervous about the future, like I was before I went into rehab, because I knew everything was going to be OK.

Money was piling into my bank account, a result of neglecting to spend close to two grand a month just feeding my addiction. Now I was able to develop a concrete plan to get nearly all my debt paid before I transitioned. I had lost a considerable amount of money a few years earlier on some investments, so I didn't have much in savings. One of my credit card companies relieved close to $10,000 in interest backdated to when I was originally issued the card. Needless to say, I didn't owe much more on that one. Coincidence or intervention? I spent a few days cleaning out my filing cabinet and several boxes wherein I had just started throwing paperwork in over the years. I still had my first pay stub, or Leave and Earnings Statement (LES), from when I initially enlisted twenty-seven years earlier. I couldn't shred all of it because the piles were massive, bordering on hoarding. Instead, I would take bags to various locations and burn them, including to my daughter's godmother's cabin up in the southern mountains of Virginia. I had endless amounts of trash, but I also found some useful, long-forgotten hidden treasures in there also, including large amounts of cash, stocks, bonds, and insurance policies, none of which I had remembered getting. It was a tremendous relief getting organized and, more importantly, getting out of debt.

I was almost done going back to work. I refused to have a retirement ceremony, as it didn't feel right and I didn't want anybody there anyway. Instead, I had a brief ceremony with my wife and daughter only. It was all the closure we needed. I only needed to get one more signature, and then turn in all my badges. I would complete this task after I got out of outpatient therapy, as soon as possible. I would be free of that place soon enough. The navy has developed a decent transition program to assist service members on their journey back into civilian life, but this is much easier said than done in most cases. It was easier for me only because I spent my last year in hospital care. Many others are not so lucky.

I learned how to write a corporate resume and focused on what I wanted to do—which was to be a plumber! I had job offers as a contractor and for government jobs, but I wouldn't have any of that. I was done with Big Brother. I did, however, learn how to write a government-service resume, just to have the knowledge. I would look back and reflect on all the government employees who had worked with and for me over the years, and I realized I wasn't willing to work with any of those knuckleheads. Government service does something to your mind and spirit, and it isn't positive. I would work myself to death doing everybody else's jobs, and that isn't how that mafia and that broken system works. I would rather be a plumber or a furniture salesman, anything but government work, and do something completely different than what I had done for twenty-eight years. It was now time to knuckle down and find out why I became an alcoholic.

CHAPTER 10
Underlying Problems

This was a difficult time, not that I hadn't already had a few of those throughout my lifetime already. I was learning to control my anger, and my first humbling experience was in rehab, where my medical technician was male, in the navy, and married to another male. I had gone my whole life outwardly disapproving this sexual preference. Since the military didn't tolerate homosexuality, neither did I. However, at this juncture in my life, I live and let live. God will sort everything out one day. Being angry or disliking someone was detrimental to my recovery, and I already had a long list that didn't need any additional names. One day at a time that would be how I will deal—with my life until I am laid to rest in my coffin, sporting my flattop.

I showed up the first day to the outpatient clinic and immediately thought I didn't belong there. My therapist was out for the first week, so I was already upset and didn't want to start repeating myself to more than one person. This is still a pet peeve of mine, and it won't get any better. After a few days, I approached the bubbly therapist who was filling in and told her I didn't belong. Apparently, this happens all the time and she smiled and asked me to sit down. She was hard not to like, and would bounce among the addicts and traumatized service members singing the theme song to "*Frozen*" and she sounded good, too. It is surprising how little things like that can cheer you up inside, but of course we couldn't show it because we were killers! She told me a story about an air-force flight-traffic controller in the desert. He got to the point where he couldn't look at the screen anymore. Seeing blips disappear on the screen eventually took its toll on him, along with all the ramifications associated with it. The loss of life, whether he knew the victims or not, didn't matter. I thought about this and reflected on my time during those rotations.

Everyone has a breaking point, and not everyone is affected in the same way. Killing isn't natural, but history has proven that it is necessary. It may not feel wrong at the time, regardless of the circumstances, but it will take its toll one day for all of us and we will be haunted and adversely affected. I had survivor's guilt, and I had become traumatized by helping all those surviving families day after day. Ok, maybe I could now use some help. The highest level of care was rehabilitation, and I needed that so I could cope and have a fighting chance at sorting out and working on my issues. Not everybody there had that opportunity, and some were dealing with their addictions fresh off their drug of choice while simultaneously dealing with all their other issues as well. I felt for them, and knew I wouldn't be strong enough to do that. There were some courageous individuals in there, a handful of whom transitioned with me from rehab to here. We had a strong bond, which would help me transition out of my community so I could deal with the "real world"; I would develop strong bonds with my new crew also.

This was the second echelon of care. I attended every day but was able to go home to my family each night. My unit was required to check on me on the weekends, but that lasted only a few weeks. I think the clinic started trusting me. My program of care consisted of treating combat trauma and substance abuse, as well as art therapy, recreational therapy, Alcoholics Anonymous meetings, and some classes offered by the post's Army Substance Abuse Program. I would end up there next, right before I signed out of active duty. That would be the lowest echelon of care, and like I stated before, I would start my career and end it there.

The first week was tough for me. It was more group-oriented because therapists are in short supply, unlike the overwhelming number of patients. I wasn't ready to talk about anything yet, at least not until my therapist showed up. I have a real problem repeating myself—must be the military training. I would be telling parts of my story to several different individuals. Nobody has heard the whole story, and it certainly isn't presented in this book. I am still waiting to tell my entire story, but it has become difficult now that I am retired. The Veterans Affairs hospital system is a government organization, enough said. My therapist did show up the second week; she was a bit eccentric but very effective.

To date, I will always remember two of my therapists. One was my substance-abuse counselor in rehab. He took every patient to heart. He spoke to my wife and daughter to get the complete picture. He was able to help me focus so I could take care of them. He was a leader among chaplains and doctors. We still speak today. The second was my trauma therapist. Therapists all had to take a unique approach with each patient; and some were certainly better than others at reaching their patients. My trauma therapist was able to reach me once I opened up. I wanted and needed help, but I still didn't know how all this mattered and played into my drinking. The structure was similar to rehab, except we were given enough rope to hang ourselves (some did).

I am proud to say that I was on the right track, soaking up everything they were throwing at me. The only one I disliked, besides yoga, was when a small electric current was applied to our earlobes, it was called cranial electrotherapy stimulator. The electrodes were attached to a small box, which regulated the intensity. It relaxed some patients, but it made me feel drunk and that wasn't what I needed or wanted. The same therapist who was recommending the electricity was also starting up a running group. She was in the air force—I forgave her for that—and she wanted to get back into shape. It was voluntary, and those who were physically able were invited. But the participants usually came down to myself and maybe one or two others. I was getting into great cardiovascular shape again, and it was a relief to be able to release some midday tension, plus it was an important part of recovery.

I spent quite a bit of time at the post USO, as it was an integral part of rehab and outpatient therapy. I would eat lunch there, attend art therapy, and take part in any other special functions they offered. This was the first time in my entire career that I had even stepped into a USO. We did continue writing, and even a few well-known authors came in and worked with us. The strangest exercise for me was the acting classes. The woman teaching them was from New York, and we went through the same exercises professional and amateur actors would pay for.

The substance-abuse portion wasn't as detailed as the program in rehab, but it did have its moments. The therapist was very nice but she certainly had her hands full with our group. We were a motley crew, ranging from old men to young mothers. This portion was less stringent, but the head of the clinic didn't mess around and expected results. He was Nigerian and didn't talk much. Patients complained about how he treated them, and I heard interesting stories about his interactions with them. But the truth was that if you were not making progress, and he suspected you were still using, then he would remove you from the program to make room for somebody who wanted to get better.

Unfortunately, that's the problem with rehabilitation and therapy, you have to want it and it is a lot of work, a big problem for some generations. Fortunately, for me, I never ended up in his office. I soaked up what I could to add to my arsenal for combating my addiction. I have lifelong friends from there, and their stories usually involved them being removed from the military or worse—their better halves leaving them. This country has a high divorce rate, and those chances are quadrupled if one or more of the partners is an addict. Luckily, I beat this statistic.

I know my recovery would have been difficult or impossible if my wife and daughter had left me. Any lesser woman would have, and I certainly wouldn't have blamed her if she did. I even talked to her about leaving me because I was in such bad shape. I was very surprised at just how bad drug addiction was across the services. This is a different generation than, say, the Vietnam era, but fifteen years of continuous war takes its toll on the best of us. There is some hard-core drug use going on, even though I almost felt my alcohol addiction was miniscule compared to others; but this certainly is not a competition. We all had problems, but just had different ways with dealing with them. If you need help, get it. Don't wait until everything spirals out of control. Be humble, hunker down, and get your issues taken care of, especially if you are in the Armed Services and still on active duty. I was lucky to get the help I needed, when I needed it, but it has been an uphill battle ever since and it will always be difficult. Having said that, my life is better now than it has ever been.

There are good days and bad days; then there are really bad days. The medication helped, but it would take a full year to get the correct combination and dosage. I was taking two or three showers a day, the heat and drumming of the water on my head helping to distract me from anxiety attacks and cravings. A few of my brethren couldn't handle the stress and anxiety associated with therapy and the cravings. Some of them would go backward in the treatment process and end up where I started in rehab. You have to get a handle on your addiction before you can start working on anything else. We were from all walks of life and different military services, but none of that mattered in that room. We were there, first, to help ourselves and in the process help each other. Some actually got the chance to be reintegrated back into their respected jobs, but for the majority of us this was it. We had to learn how to cope and figure out our new futures. I still had a urinalysis each Monday also. It didn't concern me because I was clean and sober, but not everybody was. Relapse is a part of recovery.

The trauma portion of treatment was very helpful once I knuckled down and started actually working. This therapy consisted of dealing with anger, talking about experiences, watching streaming workshops on the Internet, and creating narratives. The narrative part was a miracle. I would write down a timeline of incidents that had happened throughout my life; it was focused on combat, but some of us had deeper issues dating back to our childhoods. Then they were sequenced based on severity, and the therapist would sit down and choose which ones to work on.

Initially, the easiest one is chosen in order to get used to the process. The next step was more difficult, and I had to sequence the event on paper. There are three phases to the narrative: the first is before it happens, where the individual is in a high state of awareness; the next phase is the incident itself, where the individual reaches the fight-or-flee point; the last is sometime later, when things are calm and the individual is able to process the event. The therapist would review all this and choose the phases that would become frames. The next part was hardly the worst part, especially having been sober. I had to draw a picture of each frame. There was no limit to how many frames needed, and some people were better artists than others. This was my narrative, though, and I had to understand and explain it to the therapist. After the drawings were complete and brief notes added to each frame, I would tell my story to the therapist. Next, all the frames are attached to a white board, a camera is brought in, and they are filmed while the therapist tells me my story. It was surreal, and it would be the first time I ever heard my individual story spoken about by another person and seeing the frames. Post-Traumatic Stress Syndrome (PTSD) never goes away, but it can eventually be understood and tolerated.

I was only able to get three of these narrative completed, because it took me a few weeks to warm up to the idea that it was even necessary. I wish now that I had spent more time doing them. One was a childhood trauma, the second was an incident in

South America, and the third was during my time in a bad rotation conducting memorials, attending funerals, and helping families. These three were recorded on DVD, and are still my individual property. They are different each time I review them. I had to take everything home from all the sessions; if I hadn't, the hospital would have had to maintain them for several years since they are considered medical records. The therapists would have us review the DVDs, except that in my case, since my last one was completed on the day I was discharged, I didn't ever get a chance to review them with a therapist present. My wife sat in with me on the last one. It was very emotional for both of us.

I would move onto the post Army Substance Abuse Program and the adult mental-health outpatient section of the main hospital, and attended up until three weeks before I was retired. I wasn't getting much out of ASAP, except I did have to give periodic urine samples to prove I was still sober. This is where the chain of command would send kids after they got DUIs or had alcoholic incidents. I was doing more career counseling in there than anything else, which was great; at least I could help a few more service members not ruin their lives.

Having seen what I had seen and having been through the rehab system gave me a new perspective. In the adult mental-health section, the therapist was too overwhelmed with her patients to actually deal with my case. The initial assessment took three separate sessions. I am sure she was glad to see me go; she was new and wasn't helping me much. None of my providers, to date, ever shared any information with one another other, and that was frustrating. I was getting agitated having to tell my history over and over in bits and pieces. The nurse practitioner managed my medications, and was the only one at this point who was helping me, excepting my primary-care manager. He did an excellent job and was a good man. He even aided me when I was back down in Fayetteville, North Carolina on terminal leave by helping me to get enough of the meds I needed while I was trying to get back into the system. My PCM did everything she could to help me get my paperwork straight, and she helped me with my final physical, even getting me in to see a specialist in the traumatic brain injury (TBI) clinic. I was just able to get all the evaluations done before I signed out, and it was a good thing too, because as it turned out I had problems in that area.

I am learning how to live with my limitations by identifying them, and focusing on my strengths to overcome my weaknesses. I found out I had sleep apnea. That would explain why still couldn't get any decent sleep, even with all the pills. I was leaving Virginia with my arsenal helping me to stay healthy and alive so I could live a happy second chapter and take care of my family. Ready or not, I was transitioning into the civilian world.

CHAPTER 11

New Beginnings

never thought I could live my life without alcohol, but it became possible. I never thought there was life after the military, but there is. I never thought I could cope with trauma, loss, stress, or anxiety, but I can. I never thought I could live a life not filled with hate and anger, but I am. None of this would have been possible while still drinking all these problems away. The haze has been lifted, and I am able to move on. It certainly is not easy, and it will only get more challenging. Life mimics an oscilloscope with its ups and downs, but as long as I continue to actively seek help, things can only improve. Trusting in the path that lies before me has been a blessing, even in a world full of uncertainty.

The care I receive now is different. I am split between the active duty military hospital, the Veteran Affairs hospital, and the civilian mental-health community. At this point, I still haven't told my entire story but I am hopeful it will happen one day. Meanwhile, I am comfortably numb with all the pills the system continues to give me, a cocktail mixed with Zoloft, Inderal, and Prazosin.

I didn't know what I wanted to do upon retirement from the military, but I didn't want it to involve the government or anything that resembled what I was doing before. That revelation took a few months to come to fruition. I was given the opportunity to focus on me for once, and for that I will be eternally grateful. My outlook on life was positive, and all I needed to do was take a chance. They say that if you enjoy what you are doing, then it isn't a job. All I knew was the military, but I can safely say, after reflection, that I wasn't enjoying it after 2010 or so. I served honorably for twenty-eight years and I will leave it at that.

I am reconnecting with my family. While my social life will have to wait, I am successfully interacting with people in my current job. I have even run into a few acquaintances there. I have reconnected with my son. He is in his early twenties now, and I am so proud of him and his accomplishments. He has come out on top despite quite a bit of adversity. He has had a few run-ins with the law with some alcohol-related incidents. I can only pray that he doesn't take after his old man in that respect. I can only live my life alcohol-free and show him a better example. I will always be here for him when he needs help. He works hard and loves to fight in the local Mixed Martial Arts (MMA) circuits. He teaches wealthy knuckleheads how to defend themselves and helps coach wrestling at a private school. He has a lot of potential, and I know that he will live a long and healthy life. I know my relationship with him isn't the standard father-son duo, but I am trying to be more involved in his life. It truly is better to come through late than not to have tried at all. I have a lot of catching up to do.

My daughter was more directly affected by my alcoholism than her brother. My son's mother and I separated when he was very young, which gave me free reign to fuel my habit. He would see me get drunk every weekend, which was bad enough, but at least he wasn't watching me every day. A few years later I would remarry, and yet a few more later his half-sister would be born. I am so grateful that they had and still have an excellent relationship. That year at Fort Bliss was hell for both of them.

My daughter is adjusting well now, though, attending an excellent high school that she will actually get to attend all four years. Those in the military, past or present, know how rare that is, even in the SOF community. I am reconnecting with her and slowly building that trust back up. There is truly life after the military and an even better one sober. She is a teenager, but she clings to me like she is eight years old again. It is wonderful to have a healthy relationship with her, based on trust and love. She is a mixed pickle, as her mom is from Peru but definitely received the best attributes from both of us. She is talking about becoming a doctor one day, and I hope she does. I will support her in whatever endeavor or direction she takes in life, but it would be nice to have a physician in the immediate family to take care of my old, broken ass!

My lovely wife was born in Lima, Peru, but she is an American citizen. She is a devout Catholic and a very conservative republican. She is the best thing that has ever happened to me besides my children. I am definitely not an easy person to live with sober, and I'm infinitely worse as an alcoholic. I have enough problems to deal with, and she is the best therapy out there. She no longer has to worry about me getting drunk, urinating on friends' guest mattresses, falling down stairs, or drowning anything and everything with the bottle. I have found that there are infinite other ways to deal with my issues. She does have to deal with the nightmares, the angry outbursts, and the mood swings, but I am still sober, and she has and always will be there for me, as I will be for her when she needs me, now and forever. She is better than any drug I could ever take to calm down, and has saved my butt more than once in both my military and civilian jobs. All she has to do is talk to me over the phone, or show up and touch me and tell me that everything will be all right.

I have been a terrible son, both then and now. I would only visit my parents out of necessity, maybe once a year. I lived on the East Coast, and they lived in the Midwest. I'm not making excuses, just stating facts. I wouldn't call them or send them cards without my wife badgering me. She grew up in a culture where family is important; this country tends to look down on it. I guess I thought it was an inconvenience to stay in touch with them. This situation lasted through two marriages and all the way up to the breakdown. I haven't quite figured out why I didn't want to interact, but I was always angry. They didn't give up on me, just like God didn't, and I am glad because I need all the support I can get at this point. I suppose I blamed my mother for what I was put through and then later for what I put myself through. My second stepfather was and still is a good man, but at that point even a good example couldn't put me on the right path. I was physically and mentally abused, no doubt about it, but I still turned out all right, even after the military—just a little baggage to deal with. I didn't grow up with strong family values, but my current wife is trying to train me.

I love my mother but to this day still feel uncomfortable showing affection, and that is reciprocated. She is moving out here to be close to us, and I am still not sure how I feel about that. I was making progress with her after I sobered up, but it was from a distance, safely over the phone. I seem to be regressing again since her last visit, but I suppose that is nothing a little therapy can't fix. Mommy issues! I am getting further and further behind with my therapy, but let's see if Veteran Affairs can help me. Not!

CHAPTER 12

Why?

Why, indeed. Why am I writing this? This has been my greatest challenge—to get this story on paper. It isn't meant to make me look like a hero; on the contrary, I am the furthest thing from that. There are real heroes out there—past, present, and future. They have been, are currently, and will be in harm's way as volunteers, ensuring the population of this great nation is safe. I have had the pleasure to know many of these heroic warriors.

Maybe my story is meant to show that a spiritual awakening can happen, that it is possible to recover from anything, that one can successfully climb out of the darkest, deepest cavern—or that one slip can plummet you and everyone in range of you into hell. This book is my therapy; it is a path to a richer and fuller life. I have wronged many people over the years, and my reparations are still a work in progress. This book is my salvation, a reminder that, yes, we are all human, but we are all capable of destroying our lives and the lives of others. It is a story of where I came from and a daily reminder of how much I truly have to be grateful for and, more importantly, that the path before me is truly the right one. Only dwell on the past in order not to repeat your errors. Then move on. If I returned to my old habits, my life would be destroyed. I will not repeat that. I would die an angry, lonely old man, right up to the point where I drank myself to death.

I want to help others not to make the mistakes I made. Using alcohol and/ or drugs to hide from past, present, or future demons is not the solution. Sounds simple, right? It's not, though, even if it seems like the right thing to do at the time. Eventually you will not only destroy your life, but more devastatingly, the lives of those around you, loved ones and friends. Being an addict is a lonely life. Your whole life, schedule, and every waking and dreaming moment is spent wondering and working on how and when the next fix will come. The cries for help go unanswered to the point where, in desperation, you give your heart and soul to your addiction. It is possible not to live this way. It isn't an easy path to recover, and you can't do it alone. If you are reading this and you are not an addict, but you know somebody that is or you have a suspicion they might be, help them. The truth hurts as long as it is the truth, but just bringing the subject up might save that person's life.

I wasn't in control, and I even knew I had a problem, but it didn't matter. I knew I was slowly killing myself in front of my family, and I didn't care. I only cared about drinking until the pain went away. I made a decent living and was able to feed my habit. Always remember: there are underlying reasons why we do this to ourselves. I thought I knew why, but I was only scratching the surface.

Now that I am struggling to remain clean and sober, I have developed the ability to spot another troubled soul. It is a spiritual sense along with a few key physical attributes. These go beyond reeking of alcohol or appearing disheveled. One day I plan to help others, and I will do my best to approach and talk to anybody who is willing to listen. I now belong to two unique communities: special forces and recovering alcoholics. Each group has its unique jargon so that we can identify if someone belongs there. Unfortunately, quite a few of us belong to both groups, and many more in the first group need to belong to the second.

One day, when I am more comfortable, I will offer my help to those willing to listen in order to bridge that gap. We all need help in our lives, whether we admit it or not. If people tell you that they were able to quit on their own, congratulate them on being able to live a life free from their drug of choice, but they were either in denial, lying, or not a true addict.

Addicts are not in control of their lives; they may think they are, and I sure did, but nothing is further from the truth. I even spent money throughout the years on miraculous treatments to help me quit drinking. Some of this was on CD sets, books (other than the "Big Book"), and natural remedies. I had detoxed my body relentlessly and for naught over the years. I could have died, but some higher power had other plans for me. I would quit for short periods and then continue right where I left off, over and over. I was able to detox and stay mostly sober during combat deployments only because I knew that alcohol was waiting for me en route to my destination or at home. Addiction is a powerful and dangerous disease. I would always return to where I left off, no matter how long the dry period.

Even though relapse is part of the recovery process, I have been drinking too long and am too old for that. I don't want to die. I was very close to drinking myself to death, and I can never return there again. If you are an addict, then please get help. There are myriad resources out there that work. I can personally attest to at least three.

First, rehabilitation centers are a safe way to initially get detoxed; it is important to be monitored by health-care professionals who understand the process and who can keep you safe. Your substance of choice controls you, and it is very helpful being behind lock and key without access to it. Outpatient substance abuse therapy and counseling is the second resource. It is a more relaxed atmosphere, but you are on your own, and you must be comfortable with your coping mechanisms to fight off the cravings.

Like rehabilitation, outpatient therapy is not free or cheap, unless your health insurance covers it, but anything worthwhile usually isn't easy to access. (Make sure you research any product or facility before attending or paying, as there are lots of scams that prey on us unfortunate souls.)

The third resource I can suggest is the twelve-step program, created by Bill and Bob in the 1930s. It's absolutely free and guaranteed to work, as long as you want it to and believe it can. I believe these three methods are in the perfect order and, if followed, will guarantee a new life. All three may not be necessary, but any one of them will help you get on the right path to recovery.

Drowning your problems or putting them in an out-of-reach place is not the solution. I have a new life now, and am able to deal with the underlying reasons that brought me to eventual ruin. There is help out there.

This great nation has been in some sort of conflict ever since it was founded. It doesn't matter what the end game is, because the majority of us are true patriots and will always stand up and fight, doing anything it takes to keep any outside force (or even a subtle enemy from within) from taking that from us. Unfortunately, conflict does take its toll. Diplomacy and sanctions will never be as effective as projecting your strength anywhere there is a threat, and armed forces will inevitably be part of that package.

Killing is not natural. Witnessing death in places all over the globe, the stress of combat, seeing children perish by your own hand or another's, or feeling remorse from surviving events that took others' lives...all of this effects everybody differently. Not everyone is truthful: some do milk the system, bogging it down for those that need it, while some don't seek help and some can't get help. This is not a perfect world, and it is an even less perfect country, but we are far from being the worst. Average citizens just don't know just how fortunate they are to be here.

It may be a long and tedious process to get the help you need, but don't let that dishearten you.

www.ingramcontent.com/pod-product-compliance
Lightning Source LLC
Chambersburg PA
CBHW071416040426
42445CB00012BA/1174